Praise for SOONER FOOTBALL

"Johnny Tatum has a great understanding of football and the Sooner Nation as it stands now and over the past 50 years."
—BARB PAGE, wife of former OU QB Bob Page

"Tatum and I were teammates at OU for three years. He was a dedicated team player who showed what a young man can accomplish when he recognizes opportunity and is willing to pay the high price for success, both as a player and in a very successful career as a businessman."
—LEON CROSS, former OU assistant athletic director and former OU assistant line coach and recruiter

"Johnny Tatum, pound for pound, was the toughest football teammate I had at OU. He was also the most intense i.e. the meanest! It was important to get out of his way when he addressed the opponent's ball carrier. Just ask Jim Nance, Daryl Lamonica, Gale Sayers, or Johnny Roland. Also, Johnny Tatum had a most productive professional life, which, no doubt, can be attributed to his competitive spirit! I am proud to have been his friend all these years."
—DR. RICK MCCURDY, OU teammate and physician

"John Tatum was a leader when our football team desperately needed one. He could read individuals and motivate them to completely utilize the talent they had to offer the team. If I had to go to war, I would want John Tatum leading the way."
—DAL CAMPBELL, Okemah High School football player

"I hired this guy and when he resigned, congratulated him. On researching him, I was astonished that his grades were exceptional. He had the broadest shoulders I had ever seen and was very articulate. I pegged him as a winner and I was right. He exceeded expectations his first year as our football head coach and the second year he won our conference champion-

ship. When he resigned, I was sad but, as my best friend, I knew he could never achieve his potential as a high school teacher. So, I arranged to have a friend interview John for a job selling insurance. They hired him and, true to form, he outperformed expectations and ended up at the top of the company. John was and is the rare combination of athlete/scholar and tireless worker. I am proud to call him my friend."
—**Charles Elliott**, Radiologist & School Board President

~

On the cover of this book is the Texas High School Sports Hall of Fame halfback from Stamford, Texas, Mike McClellen. Mike played halfback for Coach Bud Wilkinson's Oklahoma Sooners in 1959, 1960, and 1961. In the cover photo, McClellen (OU #31) is tackled by a Nebraska defensive back and sent flying end over end.

Sadly, Mike McClellen passed away on June 25, 2010. So it is with great respect that we remember Mike and all the Sooner athletes who have passed away. **We are Sooner born and Sooner bred and when we die, we will be Sooner dead!**

SOONER FOOTBALL
Old School And Other Stories

SOONER FOOTBALL
Old School And Other Stories

John E. Tatum

Deeds Publishing | Atlanta

Copyright © 2015—John E. Tatum

ALL RIGHTS RESERVED—No part of this book may be reproduced in any form or by any electronic or mechanical means, including information storage and retrieval systems, without permission in writing from the authors, except by a reviewer who may quote brief passages in a review.

Published by Deeds Publishing in Athens, GA
www.deedspublishing.com

Printed in The United States of America

Library of Congress Cataloging-in-Publications Data is available upon request.

ISBN 978-1-941165-92-8

Books are available in quantity for promotional or premium use. For information, email info@deedspublishing.com.

Cover design and text layout by Mark Babcock.
OU football pictures provided by Jim Terry.

First Edition, 2015

10 9 8 7 6 5 4 3 2 1

A SPECIAL THANK YOU TO JIM TERRY

Most of the pictures included in this book were provided by popular collector of OU memorabilia, Jim Terry. Thanks, Jim—this book is much better with your pictures included.

All-American OU favorite end Tinker Owens with
OU memorabilia collector Jim Terry

TABLE OF CONTENTS

Acknowledgements	ix
Foreword	xiii
A Note From the Publisher	xvii
Introduction	xix
Comparing Old School Football to Today's Football	xxvii

SECTION ONE:
THE BUD WILKINSON AND GOMER JONES ERA
1958—1963

Getting Off on the Wrong Foot at OU	3
My First Game—Outweighed by 104 Pounds	7
Hit by a Classic "OOOOhhhh" Block	9
Becoming an O Club Member	12
The Phantom	17
Bill Hill—The Marlow Flash	20
Running Out The Clock at Mizzou—and Changing the Rules—1961	22
Johnson & Johnson All-American Team	25
The Ugh Award	27
OU vs Army—Yankee Stadium, 1961	29
Alumni Varsity Game—1963	31
Notable OU Players	34
The Exceptional Football Players We Played Against	58
1963 Orange Bowl Against Alabama	64
1950s vs Today's Football	66
The Danger of Punt Return Practice	71
OU Coaches Who Will Always Be Important to Me	74
Gomer Jones—The Great White Father's Ace in the Hole	79
Port Robertson—Mr. Discipline at OU	85
Bud Wilkinson—The Great White Father	95
A Potpourri of OU Thoughts and Stories	100

Rest in Peace	114
Was it worth it?	115
Where are they now?	119
Old School vs New School	125
Outnumbered in Nebraska	129
The Friendship of Frank and Henry	137

SECTION TWO: HIGH SCHOOL FOOTBALL THE BEGINNING OF THE COLLEGE FOOTBALL DREAM

High School Football The Beginning of the College Football Dream	142
Recruiting Formula For Playing Division I Football	143
Perfect Practice—Heed This Advice	151
The Day I Became a Coach	153
Rags to Riches at Okemah High School	160
A Coach's Impact on Boys and a Community	167
All Sports Banquet—Coach Chairbanks	169
Leaving the Job I Loved	172
My Heavener High School Teammates, An Exceptional Group of Guys	176
Carl Twidwell, My High School Coach	179
A Few More Memories from HHS	181
Some Final Tidbits to Wrap Up the High School Section	185

SECTION THREE

Sooner Magic Women	190
OU Wrestling—Mark Tatum	193
JD Roberts—A New Coach's Record Making Decision	206
Wayne Lee—Note To John	207
KJ Sanford	210
Finding Heavener, OK	212
Sooner Nation	213
About the Author	219

ACKNOWLEDGEMENTS

THANKS TO THESE FRIENDS WHO ENCOURAGED ME TO KEEP WRITING: Wann Smith, Jay Wilkinson, Leon Cross, Karl Milstead, Tom Cox, Ron Payne, Bill White, Tom Gibson, Bill Hill, Jay O'Neal, and Jerry Pettibone. And thanks to the former players at OU, Oklahoma City Star Spencer High School, and Okemah High School for their contributions to this book.

A very special thanks to my friend and unofficial Sooner historian Jim Terry for furnishing so many great photos of former Sooner greats.

Every book needs a critic who, behind the scenes, can whisper in the ear of the author valuable opinions about a word here or there, the structure of a phrase, or whether a paragraph is just too good to be in this work. That critic for this book is the very best editor I know...Nancy Tatum. She has read every word, corrected lots of sentences, and redirected many thoughts that have been written.

Bob Babcock, the CEO/founder of Deeds Publishing is tied for best editor. Bob became the best friend of the author, John Tatum, in 1947 where Bob lived across the street from Tatum at Heavener, Oklahoma. Babcock has been a diehard Sooner fan his entire life.

Writing about people you have known and loved has been a labor of love. So, good reading and onward...

JET and Nancy Jean, enjoying the Sooners
Picture courtesy of Teresa Farrington, The Okie Artist, Poteau, OK

FOREWORD

AS A YOUNG MAN, JOHN TATUM WAS AN UNDERDOG. RAISED BY HIS MOTHer, Lavelle, the family made their home in the socio-economically depressed town of Heavener in southeastern Oklahoma, just five miles from the Arkansas border. "Heavener wasn't on the way to anywhere," quipped John, "You had to specifically *intend* to go there to get there."

At the age of 11, Tatum watched a Touchdown Highlights newsreel in his local theater; it became his first exposure to football and inspired him to go out for the sport in the ninth grade. His college educated mother had been class valedictorian and had forbidden John to participate in the sport; she considered it rough, brutal, and dangerous and felt that her son would be better off devoting himself to his education. Having spent time grading papers for football players, she had developed a low opinion of their intellect and was fond of saying, "When your body's big and your brain is small, you go to school to play football." So, John Tatum, despite being considerably undersized, secretly joined the football team. The ruse succeeded until John earned a brief mention in the local newspaper's sports page, forcing Lavelle and John to reach a compromise; he was allowed to play as long as he earned no grade lower than a B in his classes.

Tatum played center and linebacker until his senior season when his coach moved him to fullback. In the fall of 1958, Heavener played Hartshorne, and Tatum turned in his best career performance. Sooner assistant coach J.D. Roberts attended the game and saw John score five touchdowns, make thirty tackles, block two punts and intercept a pass, while rushing for over two hundred yards.

John declined scholarship offers from the University of Tulsa and Oklahoma A&M (Oklahoma State today), in hopes of receiving a scholarship from Bud Wilkinson and the University of Oklahoma. Wilkinson had resisted extending the offer at first; Oklahoma was in its glory years and Bud had the pick of the regional high school talent. But J.D. Roberts was convinced of Tatum's abilities and lobbied heavily for him. In the end, Wilkinson consented and John Tatum became a Sooner.

After packing his sole possessions in a brown paper grocery bag, Tatum rode his thumb 200 miles west to Oklahoma City, Oklahoma. Once again, undersized and underdogged, Tatum over-achieved by earning significant playing time during his sophomore and junior seasons. However, the Sooners team suffered heavily from player attrition, leading to the two worst seasons in Wilkinson's tenure. But in Bud's penultimate season—and Tatum's senior season—1962, the Crimson and Cream once again rose to the top as Oklahoma posted an 8-2-0 regular season mark, won the Big 8 Conference, and earned a berth in the 1963 Orange Bowl.

Tatum graduated from OU in May 1964 and, after spending one season on campus as an assistant coach, left to become assistant football coach and head baseball coach at Oklahoma City Star Spencer High School. Tatum's 1968 baseball team won the state championship (becoming the first coach in any sport at OKC Star Spencer to win state), earning him Coach of the Year honors. In 1968, he moved to Okemah, taking over as head coach in football, baseball, and track, while teaching a full course load.

John left coaching in 1970 to enter the insurance industry with the Farm Bureau Company. He started at the bottom of the ladder as a first-line salesman and by 1988, he was appointed CEO and relocated to Lincoln, Nebraska. "I established the first OU club in Lincoln," quipped Tatum. "There was one member when I started it, and one member when I left." In 2000, four companies in an eight state area merged and Tatum retained the company-wide CEO spot. He retired shortly thereafter.

There have been many books written about football at the University of Oklahoma. Both George Lynn Cross, university president from 1943—1968, and Harold Keith, Sports Publicity Director from 1930—1969, penned erudite volumes detailing the glory years of Sooner football. But no one on the scene has been involved with Oklahoma football like John Tatum. As a young fan, as an OU football player, as an assistant coach, and as an emeritus observer, Tatum's experience, observations, comments on the current state of the football program, evaluations, and wit are enjoyed by many in his periodic email missive *Jetcetera* as well as in his first book, a biographical piece, *The Sooner the Better* (published by Deeds Publishing, Marietta, Georgia in 2006).

For insights into the OU football program, there is simply no better—or more entertaining—source than John Tatum.

Wann Smith
July 2015

A NOTE FROM THE PUBLISHER

JOHN TATUM IS MY LONGEST FRIEND—I FIRST MET HIM WHEN HE WAS seven and I was five. Even if he didn't hold the title of longest friend, I would still publish his book—it is great and one that all of us Sooner football fans will enjoy reading.

As pre-teen boys during the Korean War, John and I were always playing Army. My dad bought the two of us, plus three others in our neighborhood who played with us, WWII Army surplus helmet liners to make us 'official' Soldiers. On the back of each helmet, he painted our initials—CCO, JGB, PDT, JET, and ROB. John and I immediately declared ourselves superior, and the leaders, of our play group—our initials spelled something and theirs didn't.

From that point forward, John was JET and I was ROB—initials we proudly carry forward to this day. In this book you will see John Tatum call himself JET, John, Johnny (all his OU friends know him as Johnny), The Heavener Flash, and JETcetera (beats me where he came up with that name—but his blog about today's OU football by that title is great). All of those names refer to the same guy—my longest friend (he isn't my oldest friend, I have a great friend, Bob Turner, who was fighting for real in a tank unit in Korea while John and I were playing Army around our neighborhood in Heavener, Oklahoma).

Deeds not Words,
Bob Babcock, CEO/Founder, Deeds Publishing LLC
aka "ROB"

INTRODUCTION

Sooner Football, Old School HARKENS BACK TO MEMORIES OF A DAY WHEN Oklahoma football was a different game, played by different men than the brand played today. They wore football helmets with no face bars or just one single bar about as big around as your little finger. The rules were different. For most things that could be dangerous, there were no rules… you could block below the waist and it did not matter whether or not the player being blocked was engaged by another player. You couldn't hold, and your fist had to be next to your upper body—holding was a 15 yard penalty and a big no-no. And, there was a zone extending from tackle to tackle where it was okay to clip the defenders.

There was a sign in the training room that read, "You must be able to distinguish the difference between pain and injury!" Old School players played both ways—offense and defense. And one unspoken rule was… you had to play hurt. Targeting meant you tried to knock the ball carrier into the cheap seats, and it was legal.

Bill Hill, a meaner than a junk yard dog from Marlow, Oklahoma tells a story about Johnny Tatum and Lance Rentzel, a talented running back from Oklahoma City. The setting: slobbering Bob Ward and the Oklahoma drill. The Oklahoma drill was invented by the Great White Father (Bud Wilkinson) and his faithful sidekick, Gomer "Treadwater" Jones. (We were not sure exactly what the "T" in Gomer T. Jones was so we invented Treadwater.)

Anyway, two dummies were placed about five to seven yards apart and horizontal to each other. You had three players in the drill, a blocker, a defensive player, and a runner with the football. Who the blocker was in this situation we are remembering was lost in time and Hill, at age 73, suffers from chronic CRS. The ball carrier was future NFL star wide receiver Lance Rentzel. The defender was Johnny, you are not getting past me, Tatum, the Heavener Flash.

Bob Ward was the coach running the drill. Hill recounts the situation, "Ward wanted Rentzel to run over Tatum, but time after time, Tatum would unload on Rentzel." Ward, smelling blood and loving it, had the pair run the drill five or six times with no rest. The last time, Tatum put a form tackle on Rentzel and Lance waved the white surrender flag. Bleeding and exhausted, the drill ended with Bob Ward happier than a pig in crap!

The sight of blood meant practice was indeed Old School. And in Old School practice there was no rest break, no water, or injury time outs. There was only sweat, blood, repetition, and contact…full speed, knock their dick in the dirt contact! Oklahoma Drill!

The first time ever I saw a football game was at the Heavener Liberty Theater, part of a newsreel. In the old days, movie theaters showed a newsreel before the main show was featured. Almost no one had TV back then, the newsreel was where we saw the news. The football report was about the University of Illinois. It showed a running back for the Illini named J.C. Caroline scoring a touchdown and the crowd going wild. From that moment on, I dreamed of someday being a football player.

When I was in the eighth grade, I became the water boy for the high school football team. The school had a brand new coach, Carl Twidwell, to lead the local team…the Heavener Wolves. My father had abandoned my mother, older sister Lou, and me eight years earlier.

My mother was the Valedictorian of her high school class at DeQueen, Arkansas and a devout hater of football players. Her favorite saying was, "When your body is big and your brain is small, you go to school to play football."

So, when I entered the ninth grade and could sign up for the junior high football team, the only thing I could do was to sneak out for the team, which is exactly what I did. Coach Twidwell welcomed all of us aspiring football players to the first practice. We all gathered around him as he announced, "All of you who want to go out for quarterback come over here." Several boys declared they wanted to be a quarterback. Coach Twidwell went position by position as he asked who wanted to play each position. The last position was the center and I was the only boy left, so Coach Twidwell said, "Tatum, I guess you are our center."

Things were going really well as I loved playing my new sport. I wasn't very big for a ninth grader...I weighed in at a hefty 105 pounds. As we started playing a ninth grade schedule, I found I really liked the contact and, although I was small, I was quick and a pretty good tackler.

About halfway through the season, I played a really good game and the local newspaper, the Heavener Ledger, featured a story about our junior high football team and, unfortunately for me, I was a part of the story. When I got home that afternoon, my mom was waiting for me with newspaper in hand. When I entered the house, she held up the newspaper and said, "Now tell me about this other boy named John Tatum who is playing football. It could not be you as you were forbidden to play football."

I was caught red-handed so I confessed. My mother was disappointed in me but relented and made a deal with me. She delivered the terms and conditions in no uncertain words—I could play football as long as my grades in every class were at least an A or a B. No C or D or F's. If I failed to make the grades allowed by her deal...I would have to quit football. And furthermore, if I snuck out and tried to play without her permission, I would not like the penalty. She would enroll me in a military school! She was not going to have a dumb football player in her home. And I knew her conditions were set in granite. To me it wasn't a big deal because I actually loved school. I especially liked science and reading. My favorite classes were biology, chemistry, and general science, with English close behind.

My senior year we played a conference game with Hartshorne High School, at their stadium. It may have been my very best game ever in high school. I am not certain about these stats but they would be close to accurate. I scored five touchdowns from my position as fullback. My total offensive performance was something around 200 yards. On defense I was credited with 25 or 30 tackles, intercepted a pass, and blocked a couple of punts.

After the game as I walked off the field, a stranger came up to me and said, "Young man, I want to shake your hand. That was a great athletic performance you put on tonight." The stranger shook my hand and then disappeared into the crowd. A crowd had gathered around the stranger and me. A person from Heavener asked if I knew the stranger. I replied that I had no idea who he was. I was told it was Warren Spahn, perhaps the greatest left-handed pitcher to ever play major league baseball. And he just so happened to play for my favorite team…the Milwaukee Braves.

As great as that was to have played in front of Warren Spahn, it was another person that watched me play that was more significant. That person was a former Sooner star, an OU Assistant Coach, and Outland Trophy winner named JD Roberts. JD had travelled from Norman to watch me play. He had heard from several coaches about a talented fullback who played for the Heavener Wolves.

JD being at the game between Heavener and Hartshorne may have been the greatest single break of my life. JD became my greatest fan. It was JD who convinced Coach Wilkinson to offer me a scholarship. After much debate, JD was relentless and finally Coach Wilkinson agreed. JD came to Heavener, met with my mother and me, and signed the four-year scholarship offer. It was truly a red-letter day for me. Throughout my adult life, every time I see JD I thank him for getting me out of Heavener to OU and to unlimited opportunity.

I had proven to be a long shot athlete. I was slow to develop and, on top of that, I had suffered a plethora of illnesses. Malaria, a light case of polio, multiple allergies, and worst of all, I was a severe asthmatic. I went from 113 pounds as a sophomore to 185 as a senior. I cannot really prove it, but I am convinced that athletics was the vehicle that was responsible for my dramatic recovery. My doctor at Heavener, Dr. Gilbert Hogaboom, called me his miracle boy. With a little over one month remaining in my senior year, I became a part of the OU 1959 recruiting class.

John Tatum, Heavener High School senior fullback

JOHN TATUM

Johnny Tatum, OU center/linebacker

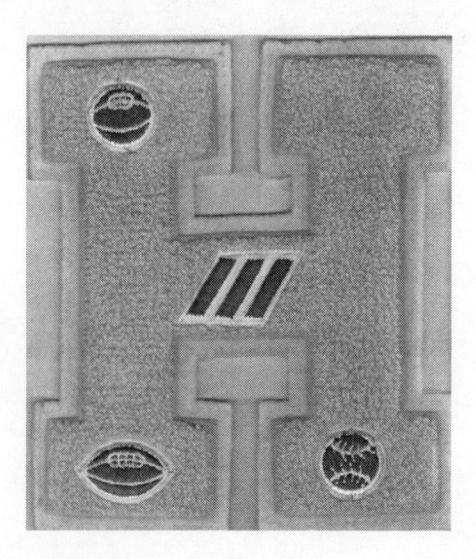

Like many boys in small schools in the 1950s, John Tatum started and lettered three years in three sports—football, basketball, and baseball.

INTERCOLLEGIATE
ATHLETICS

THE UNIVERSITY OF OKLAHOMA
NORMAN · OKLAHOMA
December 8, 1958

Mr. John Tatum
% Heavener High School
Heavener, Oklahoma

Dear John:

It was a real pleasure to meet and visit with you this past week. I am sorry that we could not have visited longer, but if you have any questions concerning Oklahoma University, please write and I will answer immediately.

Hoping to see you again real soon, I remain,

Sincerely yours,

J. D. Roberts
Ass't. Football Coach

JDR:ag

COMPARING OLD SCHOOL FOOTBALL TO TODAY'S FOOTBALL

AS BEST AS I CAN PUT IT TOGETHER, THE OU CLASS OF INCOMING FRESHmen scholarship players in 1959 was, give or take, about 45 players. A majority of those players had been high school quarterbacks or fullbacks. Four years later, only 11 of us would be remaining at OU—Monte Deere, Duane Cook, James Parker, Gary Wylie, John Porterfield, Paul Lea, Wayne Lee, Jimmy Payne, Bud Dempsey, Melvin Sandersfeld, and John Tatum. Of those, Deere, Cook, Sandersfeld, Lee, Wylie, and Tatum had earned the Letter O all three of their varsity years (remember, freshmen were not eligible for the varsity team back in Old School football days).

Often I am asked to compare Old School football at OU, played in the early days up until two platoon football gave way through the years to the current method of specialists who play only one position and situation.

Old School players were smaller, better conditioned, and football wise...smarter. This intelligence can be proven by simply looking at the degrees earned by former players. To prove my point, I will simply list the major fields of study of the 11 survivors of the freshman class of 1959. Monte Deere—Business Management, Duane Cook—Mechanical Engineering, Melvin Sandersfeld—Accounting, Paul Lea—Doctor of Dentistry, Wayne Lee—Architectural Engineer, Gary Wylie—Accounting, Jimmy Payne—Law, Bud Dempsey—Business Administration, James Parker—Business Administration, John Porterfield—Education, and Johnny Tatum—Education. And, you will notice—every surviving member of the freshmen class of 1959 graduated from college. Incidentally, Bud Wilkinson's football players graduated at a rate of 92%. Most of this statistic was thanks to the oversight of the OU Guru himself—Port G. Robertson.

It seems throughout the years when anyone engages old JET in a conversation about OU Old School football, the one thing they ask me about is the comparison of then and now...Bud Wilkinson vs Barry Switzer or Bob Stoops. Here is how I see it.

First and foremost, Bud's era players were better overall athletes. They had to be because they played both ways. Bob's players are one-way specialists...at least most of them. In Old School football, the player's offensive position dictated his defensive position and vice versa. For example, centers and fullbacks were the left and right inside linebackers in the OKIE 52 defense. Because all players had to play both ways, if a player was injured, his replacement played the same two positions as the injured player that he replaced. QBs were safeties on defense. Offensive position also dictated a player's assignment on the kick off team, the kick off receiving team, the punting team, and the punt return team. You will notice there were no specialists for the kicking game; everyone played all parts of the game.

Old School players were much more football savvy than either Barry's or Bob's boys. The Old School players were smarter players because they had to be, because of all the different assignments they were responsible for.

A huge difference in Old School football and let's say, "Modern Football," is the number of players who actually go into the game and play. In Old School football, the travelling team would have been no more than 35 or, at maximum, 40 players. Today's football team may have 50 or more players enter the game. Every situation today calls for specialists. A good example, the deep snapper on punts...most teams have one guy that snaps punts and that is all he does. In Old School football, the center did the deep snapping, snapped short snaps for extra point and field goal kicks, then did all the short snapping with the QB under center, plus played strong side inside linebacker. And, the center, as the strong side linebacker, was the defensive captain and called all the defensive signals.

Every position in the old school game had comparable assignments they had to learn in preparation for each week's opponent. It was the Tom Jones syndrome…you know…it's not unusual…that in many Old School games, only 22 players would play the entire game.

In the Old School game, each university football team had alternate starting units. In other words, two starting teams. One team would play six or seven minutes and then the other alternate starting unit would play the next six or seven minutes. That length of time was about the limit of time a player could play at an all-out pace effectively.

An opinion of the alternate unit I played on in both my junior and senior years…in both years, I felt my alternate unit was the best defensive unit and the other alternate unit was the best offensive unit. Coach Wilkinson would often call time out if the opposing team was driving the football successfully. He would send my alternate starting unit into the game and, most of the time, our unit could stop the drive. And just as obvious, the other alternate starting unit could score much easier and efficiently than my alternate unit could.

However in Bob Stoop's football world, it is all about specialists. Often a player will enter the game depending on down, distance, and field position. Everything depended upon each players skill set. For example, if it is third and eight yards to go for a first down, the defensive coordinator will substitute the cover linebacker for the regular linebacker more suited to play the run. The cover linebacker is built more like a light cornerback and more suited to cover the quicker, faster receivers in the game on third and long. Modern football of the Bob or Barry eras is more like a chess match.

On the other hand, in Bob's world of Modern Football, when a multi-position specialist becomes injured, perhaps as many as three or four players must be ready to substitute and fill the role of the injured specialist. That is why post injury, there is often confusion on the sideline. The position coaches are just trying to get the correct players into the game.

Comparing Old School football to Bob's style or Barry's style of football is like trying to compare nuclear energy to wind energy…they are both types of energy but that is where the comparison ends. Old School was real man football…well, perhaps not. If Old School was to play Modern, then who would win? It depends on which rules you would play under. The players Bob recruits are, as a general rule, much larger but probably not as fast as the smaller quicker Old School players.

But the biggest difference may be the size of player. The modern players are giants and could easily cripple the Old School smaller, no, make that much, much smaller player. I hate to say it…Bob's boys would win the game because talent usually always wins out.

When a player has to perfect one type of play and that is it, that skill is much better perfected. Therefore, because there are more skill players playing fewer minutes, the game is much better. An example of this is a statement the current OU Director of Football Operations shared with me in a conversation. Merv Johnson said, "If your offense cannot score at least 35 points, your team is going to get beat in the Big XII Conference."

Another point in this comparison of Old School and the present type of football would be nutrition. Modern players are in a whole different world when it comes to nutrition. That is why the players on the line of scrimmage are so large. Most of them are so large, heck, they could sell shade in the summertime. And one other point, they are not carrying a ton of body fat. Most of their weight is muscle. The modern players are not only larger, but are stronger and faster and more agile.

No question about it, Bob's players have better care all around than any players of any previous era have enjoyed—better medical care provided by well-educated trainers. Better nutrition delivered by professional nutritionists. Better equipment designed to do a better job of protecting the modern football player. And better pros at overseeing conditioning.

Bob's world isn't even close to looking like Bud's world. Leon Cross, one of my best friends put it this way, "Bud Wilkinson coached at OU about 15 years. Bob has coached at OU now for about 15 years. In Bud's 15th year, he was paid $45,000 dollars a year. Bob…well now it is just a tad different, sports fans. About five and a half million dollars a year. Must be inflation. That sounds like a ton of money. It is but Bob Stoops is worth every penny. The OU total sports budget is more than likely 100 million or more. While almost every form of entertainment is in decline, OU season tickets are renewing at a 96 per cent rate. A full stadium makes Bob Stoops the deal of the century.

For the last point of this comparison of Old School vs Bob's and Barry's brand of football, I will share a view given to me by my good friend, Jay O'Neal. Jay played at OU as a quarterback during the 47 straight wins era. He has the distinction of having lost only one football game in high school and college. In 1950, Muskogee defeated Ada in the semi-finals of the State playoffs and went on to win the State Championship. The Muskogee team featured future OU stars, the Burris boys, Bo Bolinger, Max Boydston, Joe Rector, and a future All American end named Carpenter who played for Arkansas. The next year, they moved up a class and did not play Ada again. In 1952, Seminole brought their single-wing offense to the Ada game and it proved to be unstoppable. Seminole accomplished the unthinkable in a regular season game, they handed Jay O'Neal his lone defeat in his entire playing career. But Ada went on to win the State Championship in 1952, with Jay O'Neal at quarterback.

Jay had this to say about Old School vs today's football, "The offensive lines ability to use their hands in blocking is a huge difference. Also, the tackles can line up off the line of scrimmage. The officials let them get as deep off the line of scrimmage as a slot back or wing back. It is a huge advantage in pass blocking. In addition, the receivers can run uninterrupted down field. This makes all receivers extremely difficult to cover. And today's coaching staffs have many more coaches than Old School staffs had—seven assistants in 1962, Wilkinson, Jones, Feldman, O'Neal, Crowder, Ward, and Franklin."

This book is about the Bud Wilkinson and Gomer Jones era of Old School football. For us old timers, we remember those glory days from growing up as Bud and Gomer were building the 47-game winning streak that still stands today. For those of us fortunate enough to have played at OU in the Wilkinson/Jones era, it is a major highlight in our lives—both then and now as we look back on it.

For you younger Sooner fans who didn't live with the Sooners each Saturday in the fall of the 1950s and early 1960s, here are just some of the Great White Father's accomplishments:

Three national championships in 1950, 1955, & 1956
31 consecutive victories 1948-1950
Scored in 123 consecutive games 1947-1957
Won 12 consecutive conference championships
47 consecutive victories 1953-1957 (a record that still stands)
Bud's record was 145-29-4 (.833%)
And a graduation rate of 92%

Jay O'Neal #17, OU Quarterback who lost only one game in his junior high, high school, and Sooner years.

JOHN TATUM

Bud Wilkinson hugs QB #12 Monte Deere

SECTION ONE
SOONER FOOTBALL: OLD SCHOOL
THE BUD WILKINSON AND GOMER JONES ERA
1958—1963

GETTING OFF ON THE WRONG FOOT AT OU

DEAN BASS FROM NEARBY MOORE, OKLAHOMA, DON DICKEY FROM PHILlips, Texas, and John Tatum from Heavener, Oklahoma made history just a short while after arriving for their freshman year as student/athletes at OU. Bass and Dickey were running backs and Tatum was a center/linebacker. It was just a few days from the Red River shootout…the Texas-OU game in Dallas, Texas.

Port G. Robertson had given his "this is how you are to behave" talk for those freshmen who would drive the three plus hours to Big D for the game on Saturday afternoon at the Cotton Bowl stadium. In his talk advising the freshmen on the do's and the don'ts, he had a stern warning about scalping tickets. Honestly, I had no idea what that meant…scalping tickets. I had grown up in a small town located at the foothills of the Ozark Mountains. Heck, I thought the name of my hometown was "Resume Speed" until I was in high school. After all, Resume Speed was the only sign on the highway heading out of town!

Scalping tickets…no one from Heavener ever heard of such a thing. When Port Robertson said scalping tickets, I thought perhaps he was referring to some Indian ceremony! The three of us arrived in Big D at about 7 pm and decided to stop at a local downtown restaurant and eat a burger and fries. We had just settled down at the bar in the diner when Dean Bass whipped out two Texas-OU tickets, "I've got two Texas-OU tickets on the 50 yard line," Bass yelled.

Quickly a local patron, dressed up in a suit and tie, asked, "Where are the tickets located in the stadium and what do you want for them?"

Bass shot back, "They are on the 50 yard line and I want 25 dollars each."

The stranger nodded and said, "I will take them but I have to step around the corner and get my money from my room," and he disappeared. In the meanwhile, the three amigos downed their sandwiches and fries. When Bass had finished, he handed Don Dickey the two tickets and said, "I need to go to the bathroom, here are the tickets, when the man returns, give him the tickets, and get my fifty bucks."

No sooner than Bass had gone to the bathroom, the stranger reappeared, Dickey gave him the two tickets, and the stranger handed old JET the money, entrapping both Dickey and me.

Faster than a hiccup, the stranger whipped out a Dallas policeman's badge and said, "You two are under arrest for scalping tickets." All of a sudden I knew what scalping meant. It was not good news to be so well informed.

Off the two of us went, under arrest. Bass came out of the bathroom and said, "Hey, wait on me." It was a good news bad news deal…the bad news…Dickey and Tatum were going to spend the night in jail. The good news, Dickey and I set a new OU record for going to jail in the quickest amount of time for the Texas-OU weekend. We had arrived in Big D at 7 pm and the two of us were in jail at 8:15 pm.

Dean Bass had the pleasure of calling Port to get Dickey and me out of jail. We were out just in time to make it to the Texas—OU game at about 12:45 pm and watch the opening kickoff. The OU players had already heard about our misfortune. On the sidelines during the game, varsity players would come over to Dickey and me and say, "Hey, you dumb ass freshman, do you know what kind of a bird doesn't fly? A jail bird." If we heard that once, it was a hundred times over the next few days. But little did we realize, the real hard times were in store for us the moment Port entered the game Dickey and I had started on Friday night. And Dean Bass was on our sh*t list, big time.

When I arrived Saturday evening back in Norman, there was a note on my dorm room, "Be in my office at seven Monday morning, Mr. Johnny Edward Tatum…signed PGR."

Port was already in his office and ready to deal with the three of us. When Port was finished, I went back to my dorm room. My roommate, Max Morris, a senior majoring in Electrical Engineering asked me how my meeting with Port went. I told Max, "Port said he was going to take us under his wing." I asked Max what that meant. Max said, "It means you had better clean this room from top to bottom before Port checks our room at noon."

I did what Max told me to do. The room was spotless. When Port arrived, he did a white glove examination. I smiled inwardly, it looked like I had won round one against Port. He looked disappointed as he headed toward the door of my room, when all of a sudden, Port stopped and, like a bird dog, turned and pointed to a bottle of aspirin I had in the corner of my book shelf. "Are these your aspirins, Mr. Tatum?" Port asked.

I said they were and asked if you couldn't have aspirins in your room. Port's response turned my smile upside down into a frown. "Sure you can have aspirins, Mr. Tatum, but just look at these aspirins. They are a symptom of your problem. You are a messy disorganized person; the aspirins in the bottle are not stacked up one on top of another. Mr. Tatum, the way I see it, you, Sir, will owe me 100 stadium steps. I will see you in the morning at 6 am on section 3 and 4!"

Now for the record...two things. One stadium step was from the bottom Row 1 to the top of Owen Stadium Row 72, and when PGR blew his whistle, you had to run up the stadium and be at Row 72 in 15 seconds or it did not count. In excellent physical condition, you could run 10 steps in one session. So, it would take me at least 10 days to run 100 steps. Now for the other record...Don Dickey, my roommate our sophomore year, and old JET set a record in Big D for being arrested in the least amount of time, a record that has stood for 56 years as of the writing of this book. (2015)

Sadly, Dean Bass left the team. I do not know why. I have not seen or heard from him since 1960. My roommate, Don Dickey, was injured and due to a serious knee injury, he left the team early in 1961. He did graduate with a degree in Mechanical Engineering. He lived and worked in the metropolitan Dallas Ft. Worth area until his death in his sixties. Don was a great guy and a really good running back with superior speed.

In another part of this book I detail just how Port and I got along after such a tumultuous beginning my freshman year. Port did not know this but he could not run me off because I had no place to go. My new stepfather was an alcoholic. He and I had gotten into an actual fistfight about two weeks before I graduated from high school. I left Heavener the day after graduating and never lived at my mother's house again.

MY FIRST GAME—OUTWEIGHED BY 104 POUNDS

IT WAS TWO WEEKS BEFORE THE 1960 OU FOOTBALL SEASON OPENER. Northwestern University was in Norman to play the Sooners. Two-a-days were over and it was time to focus on Northwestern. Bob Ward had put photos of the player we would be across from above our lockers. It was the first time I had ever heard of Fate Echols, the mammoth Northwestern defensive tackle. Bob Ward had written, "This is Fate Echols, intimidate him!" Under the photo of old Fate were his particulars—6'4" 285 pounds! I did some quick math...let's see, I weigh 181 and my height is 5'10" so this guy I am supposed to intimidate is six inches taller than me and outweighs me by only 104 pounds!

When game time finally arrived, my Sooners won the toss and elected to receive. Our starting unit was brilliant and marched right down the field, stalling out inside the ten yard line. Coach Wilkinson called me up and said, "Tatum go in and tell Milstead to kick a field goal." Old JET was the alternate starting unit right guard, playing behind Junior Karl Don Milstead, from Athens, Texas.

Wearing home Crimson number 64, old JET made his first ever varsity football appearance on the hallowed turf of Owen Field (John was a guard his sophomore year before moving to center and #50 his next two years). I handed the kicking tee to the quarterback and broke the huddle with the extra point kicking team. As I arrived at the line of scrimmage, I was face to face with Fate Echols, whom I was supposed to intimidate. Our quarterback and signal caller began to call the snap count..."hut one, hut two, hut three..." and with each count Fate Echols drew his forearm back one more notch. Finally, the ball was snapped...the last thing I remember was doing somersaults through the air.

When I awoke, I was sitting on the kicking tee and the referee was signaling Milstead's kick was true to his mark...Good! OU led 3-0. It was our only score that day, but it would not be the only butt kicking Fate Echols would administer on me. My cat like quickness would save my life. I wondered if I was cut out to play big time college football. My first outing left me wondering if perhaps my mother, Lavelle, had been right, "When your body is big and your brain is small, you go to college to play football."

Well, sports fans, compared to old Fate I was a small fry and my brain...arguably large enough to be anything but small. I knew if I was going to survive, it would be because of one asset old JET brought to the table...my cat like quickness and meaner than a junkyard dog!

HIT BY A CLASSIC "OOOOHHHH" BLOCK

ISN'T IT JUST WONDERFUL TO BE ALIVE! I THINK THAT EVERY MORNING when I wake up. And it is all because of a rather unruly fellow I encountered back in the fall of 1961. His name…Bob Brown. Bob Brown played tackle for the Nebraska Cornhuskers. Hell, let's just tell it like it is…Bob Brown was the Nebraska Cornhuskers. Mr. Brown, as I very early on referred to him, is arguably the greatest lineman ever to wear the Red and White of NU. He stood about 6'4" and was about a biscuit under 300 pounds. I played across from him on both offense and defense. It proved to be a very long day in Lincoln.

Nebraska jumped out to a 14-0 halftime lead. Our Sooners were lucky it wasn't 30-0 at the half. Our coach, Bud Wilkinson, went ballistic in the Sooner halftime locker room. He let us know, among other things, that our gender was somewhat in question. And in no uncertain terms we were told how we were a disgrace to the Crimson and Cream uniforms we wore. Perhaps the worst part of the Great White Father's tongue lashing was the regret he felt to be seen in public with this OU football team since we were totally devoid of any character or grit. At the height of his oratory, the referee interrupted coach with the five minutes until kickoff warning.

Coach Wilkinson turned to his right hand man, Gomer Jones, perhaps the greatest offensive and defensive line coach in the world, and said, "Gom, give me a five minute head start and then you bring out these ladies." Ronnie Payne, our big tight end from Breckenridge, Texas rose as if by command and yelled out, "Come on you guys, let's go out there and kick their ass." Coach Wilkinson swung around and snapped, "Sit down and shut up, Payne. That is the trouble with this team…you are all talk and no action!"

I can still recall my feelings as I sat there in the locker room in Huskerland, fully knowing I had just heard a "rah, rah, rah, let's go get 'em" halftime talk delivered by the Great White Father. I knew that…but I also was bleeding from almost every orifice on my poor beaten body. In the first half, Mr. Brown had come close to having been charged with assault and battery with a strong intent to kill…ME!

During the game, it was my duty to do all of the long snapping. I snapped on extra points, field goals, and punts the entire game. My blocking assignments were as follows. If I was covered by a Nebraska player, then I would snap the football and become a second safety in the punt coverage. On extra points and field goals, I would snap the ball and block as best I could. But on punts, if I was uncovered, I would snap the ball and release down field and be the first OU player down field on punt coverage.

Now for the first three quarters, I had been covered. But on our first punt in the fourth quarter, bingo, I was uncovered. So, I snapped the ball and released downfield with my eye on the NU deep back, Willie Ross. Willie caught the ball and I was just a bit too far from him…about five yards. Willie faked to his left, my right, and broke me down. Then Willie headed for the east sideline and wanted to turn the corner and head north toward the end zone. I knew I must tackle Willie before he turned the corner or I would become the post block on the NU punt return.

I took what I thought was a great angle of pursuit and kicked in the old Tatum cat-like quickness. But lo and behold, Willie had gazelle type speed and beat me to the corner. All I remember is seeing number 62 coming full speed toward me. It was Mr. Brown. I quickly made the sign of the cross and muttered to myself, "Those of us about to die salute you." I had seen these things done in movies with scenes where someone's death was impending.

Now folks, Bob Brown hit me with a classic "OOOOhhhh" block. For you unsophisticated footballers, an "OOOOhhhh" block is when one is hit so hard all the fans simultaneously go, "OOOOhhhh." I can still remember hearing the "OOOOhhhh's" as I came down from my half gainer position in the air. You know, head first...feet up in the sky. I hit the ground in front of our OU bench. Everyone in Nebraska's Memorial Stadium knew I was hurt. The question was—how badly?

The first thing I remember was hearing the Witch Doctor's voice saying, "Johnny, are you alright?" We all affectionately referred to our head trainer, Kenny Rawlinson, as the Witch Doctor. Finally my brain registered Kenny's voice and my first response to him was, "Kenny, I am not alright at all. I am blind in the right eye, Kenny, I cannot see anything!" I heard Kenny sort of chuckle. Immediately I said, "Kenny, this is not a funny situation at all." All I could think about was how, for so many years, all of my coaches had lied to me. Even beginning with Bob Terry, my junior high coach, who told me, "Johnny, keep your eyes open, no one has ever been blinded in football." My high school coach, ditto; my college coaches, ditto. Now I sat there in enemy territory, blind in the left eye!

Kenny retorted, "Johnny, I think you are alright. Can you sit up?" I acknowledged that I could. I righted myself and Kenny straightened out my headgear. The force of Bob Brown's hit on me spun my helmet on my head so that one of my eyes was completely covered and the other one was looking out an ear hole. I am here to tell you if you have ever been hit like this, then every day you live is a great day to be alive.

As a footnote and fitting epilog to this story. The Sooners of '61 snatched victory from the jaws of defeat and won the game in Lincoln, Nebraska 21-14. Once again, Sooner Magic prevailed. In the Sooner locker room, Coach Wilkinson would tell us what great courage we had and about the character we each possessed to rally from defeat and win the game and how we were building on the great Sooner tradition. It is truly remarkable what thirty minutes of winning football can make in one's character, especially when you come from behind and win.

BECOMING AN O CLUB MEMBER

Note to Readers: Do not attempt any of this at home. The antics and events related to the annual O Club initiation have long been outlawed by the University of Oklahoma. Starting in the 1960s, common sense prevailed and OU and most universities eliminated the potentially dangerous activities from all organizations on campus—athletic clubs, Greek organizations, etc.

ONE OF THE REAL SPRING HIGHLIGHTS AT OU WAS THE ANNUAL O CLUB initiation. This was an ordeal held usually the first Friday after spring football was over. It was an all day deal for first year O Club Letter winners in all sports.

The torture began at daylight. All the new soon to be O Club winners would arise at 6 am for a morning run through the Duck Pond on the old golf course. Then each would be clad in an OU tee shirt on backwards and inside out, shorts worn the same manner…inside out and on backwards, and tennis shoes. A string ran from your crotch to just out of the neck hole on your tee shirt. The string had a pencil tied to the end of it. The other end of it was attached and tied to your Willie.

During the day, all initiates would have to have each of their college professors sign the placard that hung from your neck proclaiming, "I AM AN O CLUB ANIMAL". The varsity cheerleaders also signed, as well as all O Club members. Each signature was indeed an experience, as the signers didn't know what the string was anchored to.

Late in the afternoon all candidates assembled in Owen Stadium for the final ceremony. The public was banned from attending. I should state for the record before proceeding any further, this ritual has long since been discontinued at OU—and rightfully so. But back in the old days when it happened, it made for some memories that lasted lifetimes.

Wesley Skidgel was a hardnosed red headed knock you into next week defensive back and halfback from Tulsa. For a back, Skidgel was tough as they come. I always liked Wes, he was an easy guy to like, despite being so tough. Wes and I were talking about it only a few days from the initiation. The initiation's worst was the first station…the atomic balm ointment liberally splashed on one's genitals and rubbed under the arm pits. It would set you on fire and make you miserable for about an hour.

I told Wes, "When you come down the ramp you will have a sack over your head and you will be stopped at the atomic balm station. Just yell out, 'hey it's me, Wes,' and we will know it's you and act like we are pouring on the atomic balm and you can act like you are rubbing it in and it is burning you so scream real loud." So, old Wes did his part exactly like we rehearsed. What he did not know was that someone at the atomic balm place put a black X on the back of Wes's sack. When everyone had gone through the atomic balm station, we had about a gallon and a half remaining. So, we began a search and destroy mission looking for a sack with a black X on the back. Bingo, we found him and commenced to pour the remaining gallon and a half of liquid heat on the unsuspecting Wesley Skidgel.

After the initiation was over, we were enjoying our favorite libations at Louie's Library and Tutor Service when Wes recounted his ordeal with the atomic balm. He thanked us for sparing him but then quickly added that some SOB had poured at least five gallons over him later. We all couldn't believe someone would do such a dastardly deed, as we grinned like the cat that just ate the canary.

The all-time best O Cub initiation story came during one of the famous "Marshmallow Races." This event was held with six to eight participants per heat with the race run in heats. The participants ran the race in the reverse crab position, on their back, hands and feet on the ground with their abdomen pointed toward the sky. They had on nothing but a jock strap and sack over their head. Each participant had to carry a marshmallow. The only place to carry it was, naturally, the crack of their butt.

The race instructions each group heard were, "Gentlemen, this is the famous O Club Marshmallow race. The object of the race is simply not to be the loser because the loser has to eat the winner's marshmallow." Everyone got it…just do not lose. So the whistle was blown and off went the wanna be O clubbers. Sure enough, the guy we had selected to lose, lost the race.

While he was being harassed and occupied with never ending distractions, someone at the finish line took a new marshmallow out of the bag, put it on a stick and rubbed it in the grass to make it look more authentic. He brought the marshmallow back and said to our loser, "Here is the winner's marshmallow, now eat it 'cause you lost the race fair and square."

The losing wanna be O clubber flatly refused to eat the marshmallow…several times. Finally one of the coaches overseeing the event came over and inquired as to what the ruckus was all about. We told him that the candidate had lost the marshmallow race fair and square and refused to eat the winner's marshmallow.

This coach epitomized tough, so he looked at the candidate and asked if that was right? The candidate said, "That's right, Mr. Coach…I ain't eating the winner's marshmallow, but I will eat mine," and down the hatch it went. We were all down on the ground laughing.

When the O Club initiation started at 6am, all of the candidates were given methyl red or methyl blue diuretics. So, all day you would urinate either red or blue. That was a real treat to belly up to a urinal in the student union with about 20 other guys and let loose a stream of red or blue urine. Talk about clearing out a restroom in a hurry.

Some of the rituals were over the top, but most of it…at the time… was something to laugh about later. In the decade of the seventies, the O club initiation was done away with, for good cause. It was at least a minor miracle that some athlete did not die. If it was not the worst day of my short life, it was in the top three!

FOURTEENTH ANNUAL BANQUET

VARSITY

O

CLUB

May 16, 1961 — 6:30 p.m.

UNION BALL ROOM

Student Union Building — University of Oklahoma

Norman, Oklahoma

NEW LETTERMEN OF 1960-1961
(Continued)

1960 FOOTBALL

Duane Cook	Dale Keadle	Dale Perini
Leon Cross	William Lee	Elton Dale Salmon
Monte Deere	Billy Meacham	Melvin Sandersfeld
Donald Dickey	Brent Morford	John Tatum
H. O. Estes	James Parker	Bill Winblood
Claude Hamon		Gary Wylie

1961 SWIMMING

Benno Fischer	Gerrit Maris	Hal Williams
	Bob Reese	

1960 TENNIS

1960 TRACK

Mark Brady	Tom Raley	Buddy Stewart
David Ewing	Dick Sinclair	Don Warrick
Robert Knight	Lee Smith	Robert Wilcox
Walter Myers		Ralph Youngworth

1961 WRESTLING

Wayne Baughman	Wally Curtis	Von Henry
Bill Carter	Bob Deupree	Phil Keeley
Joe Chamberlain	Tom Edgar	Mickey Martin
	Joe Gibson	

THE PHANTOM

MY CAREER AT OU WAS A VERY FAST FIVE YEARS—FOUR YEARS AS A PLAYER and one year as a graduate assistant. The friends I made in those five years were special and many have persisted throughout my life and many have become stronger through the years. But in this book, I am only going to write about the real characters. There were many.

One of the most unforgettable characters was my roommate, John Porterfield. John hailed from Bixby. I nicknamed him the Phantom. We took it upon ourselves to oversee the freshmen each year, to sort of show them the ropes, so to speak, and to make them feel welcome and be a part of the team at OU. One of the first lessons we would need to teach them all was to keep their room locked.

One incoming class had these two freshman…damn freshman that is to say…named Jerry Hayden and Ron Harmon. These two extraordinary dudes needed to be taken under the Phantom's wings…and they were. One day their room was unlocked and open. And as luck would have it, the Phantom had been duck hunting with his faithful sidekick, the Heavener Flash. Stumbling upon a bunch of cattail reeds was about as lucky as you could get. So, we seized the opportunity and harvested as many as we could carry. Intuitively, the Phantom just knew the right situation would present itself for the cattails to become an important teaching aid for a couple of damn freshmen. It only took about five minutes for said opportunity to present itself after we had arrived back at the Animal House…aka Washington House, the athletic dorm.

Here is the situation. These two damn freshmen, Haydon and Harmon, had a giant fan in their room. The Phantom positioned the fan right at the doorway into their room and turned it on low. Then the Phantom began beating the cattails on the rim of the fan. In no time at all there must have been a foot deep of cattail fuzz in their room. Then the Phantom shut their door and left his calling card, "You damn freshmen should keep your door locked." It was signed, The Phantom.

Although I personally knew who the Phantom was, in all our years at OU, I never once disclosed it, not even once. To all others, Porterfield and Tatum were known as the "Onagers." And everyone knows an Onager is a Wild Ass from the East. We would do our laundry about every month or so, mostly when we were out of clean clothes to wear. When we were at the local laundry mat and our clothes were in the dryer, I informed my roommate, the Phantom, that I was colorblind and would he be so kind as to sort my socks for me. This would prove to be a huge mistake in the making. John Porterfield was not to be trusted with this sort of information. He sorted my socks alright, by putting a green sock with a red one…in fact not even one of my socks was with its mate. I spent the next month having coeds point out that my socks did not match.

The only thing left for me to do, get even with the Phantom! So, occasionally after the Phantom dropped off to slumber land, I would get up, find his three tooth upper partial plate and hide it. He would attend class for a few days with no front teeth. A peace treaty would ensue after he agreed to match my socks!

I once saw a movie about Jesse James. In the course of the movie it was disclosed Jesse and his gang were getting credit for many bank robberies someone else actually committed. The same factoid held true at Wash House. Many evil deeds were blamed on the Phantom. And the truth be known…he and his faithful sidekick, the Heavener Flash, were as innocent as the driven snow.

One particularly dastardly deed happened late one night when a stumpy guard named Jimmy Gilstrap arrived back at Wash House, shall we say inebriated. Actually according to most accounts, Gilstrap was falling down drunk. He was so drunk he could not have found his own ass in a hundred grabs. So, some group of yahoos took Gilstrap to the showers and proceeded to shave every hair from his body. Then the cowards blamed it on the Phantom and his trusted sidekick, the Heavener Flash. All I can say here is, "Not Guilty."

The Phantom and I were innocent. Here is the ironclad alibi, Gilstrap was a sophomore. The Phantom and the Heavener Flash only worked with and trained the damn freshmen who needed help in adapting to college life in an athletic dormitory. And I state emphatically this irrefutable fact…what the Phantom and his trusted sidekick did was done for the damn freshmen's own good. And as Archie Bunker would say, "Case closed."

John Porterfield—The Phantom

BILL HILL—THE MARLOW FLASH

ENOUGH ABOUT FRESHMEN. LET ME TELL YOU ABOUT THE MARLOW FLASH, Bill Hill. Bill played offensive and defensive tackle. He was the first football player I ever knew that played using Braille. Bill Hill was, for all intents and purposes, blind when he took off his glasses, and he played football without glasses. Therefore it would follow Bill Hill played the game and couldn't see diddly squat.

When I was a senior we were playing Colorado at Boulder. OU was beating the crap out of the Buffalos. I was in the game, OU was on defense. Bill Hill was in at defensive tackle. Colorado was running a wide play to our defensive left side and I was playing linebacker on the left side. I had established a perfect inside out angle of pursuit on the Colorado back carrying the mail. Our defensive end, John Flynn, from Washington, DC, had perfect containment on the runner.

I knew when the running back reached the sideline, he would have to cut back to the inside and I would knock his scrotum in the dirt. Just as the Colorado Buff running back cut back, I was clipped big time. I ended up in a pile of players. So, I just grabbed the nearest Colorado player by the facemask and began punching him. I must have hit him six or seven times before the referee grabbed me and said, "Number 50, you are out of the game!" It was the only time in all the years I had played football that I had been thrown out of a game. And to my knowledge, this was the only penalty ever called on me personally. I knew the Great White Father would take a very dim view of this failure on my part to "keep my poise."

After the game I was standing in the shower, trying to cool off, when I heard Bill Hill interrupt the sound of the cool water splashing on my beat up body. "Johnny," Bill began, "do you know that Colorado guy you were punching. Well he was not the guy who clipped you." Bill Hill looked a little bit like Mr. Magoo without his glasses on. I retorted, "Oh yeah, well how do you know it wasn't him, Bill?"

In his slow Marlow drawl, Bill said, "Cause it was me…I was zeroing in on hitting this Colorado guy and missed him and hit you." I just sort of grinned at Bill's admission of guilt. Hell, it made sense, the guy was blind. Heck, when Bill had his glasses on, his lenses looked like the bottom of two coke bottles.

Bill Hill went on to become a Colonel in the US Army. And get this, he was in Intelligence. He rode around in a B-52 looking for someone to bomb. When Bill told me this at a reunion after he had retired from the military, I thanked him for not having told me earlier what he did in the service. I could not have nor would I have been able to go to sleep knowing the Marlow flash was actually in charge of aiming a bomb anyplace.

RUNNING OUT THE CLOCK AT MIZZOU—AND CHANGING THE RULES—1961

OKLAHOMA, A THREE-TOUCHDOWN UNDERDOG, UPSET THE FAVORED TIgers on a misty rainy day on their home field in Columbia, Missouri. One year earlier, in Norman, Mizzou had humiliated OU with a 41-17 blowout as my former teammates from Heavener High School watched from the bleachers in the south end zone. It was the most points scored on us in a game during that dismal 3-6-1 season.

Late in the game, OU faced a fourth and long situation with about a minute and a half remaining in the game. Johnny Tatum, the center, held the ball and did not center it, running valuable time off the game clock. The play clock expired and the referee penalized the Sooner offense five yards for delay of the game.

The ref marched off the five-yard penalty and started the clock. Again Tatum did not snap the ball to the OU punter, Ronnie Payne. When the play clock expired again, the ref marched off another five-yard penalty and again started the clock. This time the game clock ran all the way down to zero and OU was successful in upsetting the heavily favored Missouri Tigers, 7-0.

The win was huge for Oklahoma and Coach Bud Wilkinson, who would later categorize this game as one of the biggest victories for his Sooners. The Missouri head coach, Dan Devine, was, to say the very least, livid over the manner in which the Sooners had manipulated the game clock in the waning moments of the fourth quarter.

In fact, Devine led a movement at the winter meeting of the NCAA rules committee to change the rule on dead ball fouls. He was successful as the new rule adopted was that on dead ball fouls the clock would stop and not start again until the ball was snapped.

Johnny Tatum has that game football. It is on display at the Norman Legends Motel located off I-35 and Lindsey Street in SW Norman. Coach Wilkinson proclaimed that Johnny Tatum was not one of the greatest OU centers ever, but certainly one of the most intelligent.

The OU victory started a string of wins for OU that culminated in the Sooners winning the Big 8 Championship the following season. The Sooners went undefeated in Big 8 conference games from the Missouri win throughout the 1962 season. It was Coach Wilkinson's last conference championship.

An epilog on the Sooner win over Misssouri. The week of practice before the OU game with the Missouri Tigers was a disaster for the OU alternates. The screw-ups started in the all-important Tuesday practice. It seemed everyone had their heads up their butts. Linemen couldn't successfully execute the snap count, backs would hit the wrong hole and fumble the ball, and receivers would drop passes. It was, to say the very least, a disastrous performance by the alternates.

It seemed impossible the execution could get any worse, but it did. Wednesday's practice was, in a word, horrible. It was Tuesday except to the tenth power worse. Thursday was so bad that Bud stopped practice and demoted the alternates to the last team. He made us repeat practice and told us he wished he could leave us at home, but it was too late.

We got to Missouri and the game. OU lost the toss and Bud blamed that on the alternates for the way we had practiced. When the game started, MU drove the ball down to the four-yard line and Bud called time out. He called us up to the sideline and put us in the game and said, "Let them score on you because of the way you practiced."

We went in the game and held them on four tries. The Green Bay Packers could not have scored on us. After the game we were out of Bud's doghouse. My alternate unit teammates played lights out in the Sooners victory over MU that day in Columbia. We found our poise and determination and we were once again men with great heart and courage. Boomer Sooner. And we had revenged the butt-kicking we received from Missouri in 1960.

JOHN TATUM

The next season, in Norman playing in front of our largest crowd of the season (except for the annual Texas game in Dallas), we defeated a tough Missouri team 13-0.

OU alternate Center Johnny Tatum, #50, zeros in on Missouri QB Ron Taylor running an option play against Tatum and the Sooners. Tackle Duane Cook, #72, comes in to help.

JOHNSON & JOHNSON ALL-AMERICAN TEAM

THROUGH THE YEARS, THE PEOPLE I HAVE COME TO KNOW THROUGH WORK or friendships have shown an amazing interest in the fact that I was a football player for Bud Wilkinson's Sooners. When introduced by this same group of friends I have often been introduced as a former Sooner All American. The only All American team I was ever named to was the Johnson & Johnson All American team. To this team, I was a consensus three-time All American. This team was made up of the football players who used the most tape and protective equipment in order to be able to play in the game.

I believe it took the Witch Doctor the better part of thirty minutes to get me taped up to either practice or play. He taped both of my knees, both ankles, and made a special little cast for one of my fingers which was broken. I wore special reinforced shoes to prevent high ankle sprains and wore a set of shoulder pads reinforced in the front to protect my separated sternum. Other than that, I was good to go. In three years of varsity football at OU, I had knee surgery four times and nose surgery once. I could have played in 31 games and played in 26.

In my four years at OU I should have been awarded at least 46 Purple Hearts for having been wounded in action. I lost six and a half teeth, broke three ribs, separated my sternum, four knee surgeries, one nose surgery, several concussions, a couple of broken fingers, multiple sprained ankles, a broken left foot, and a severely damaged self image. I did not understand at the time these injuries would be just a partial payment for the "free college education" I was receiving at OU. As I would age, the repayments of my "free" college education would increase as one of the bill collectors I call one of the "itis" boys would come calling. His first name…Arthur. Yep, old Arthuritis. In the hands, shoulders, feet, and back.

My mother actually had envisioned me playing in the high school band. She wanted me to be a band weenie. I should have listened. Even better, I should have been a male cheerleader. Just imagine a life without arthritis. Oh what the hell, back to the funnier stuff.

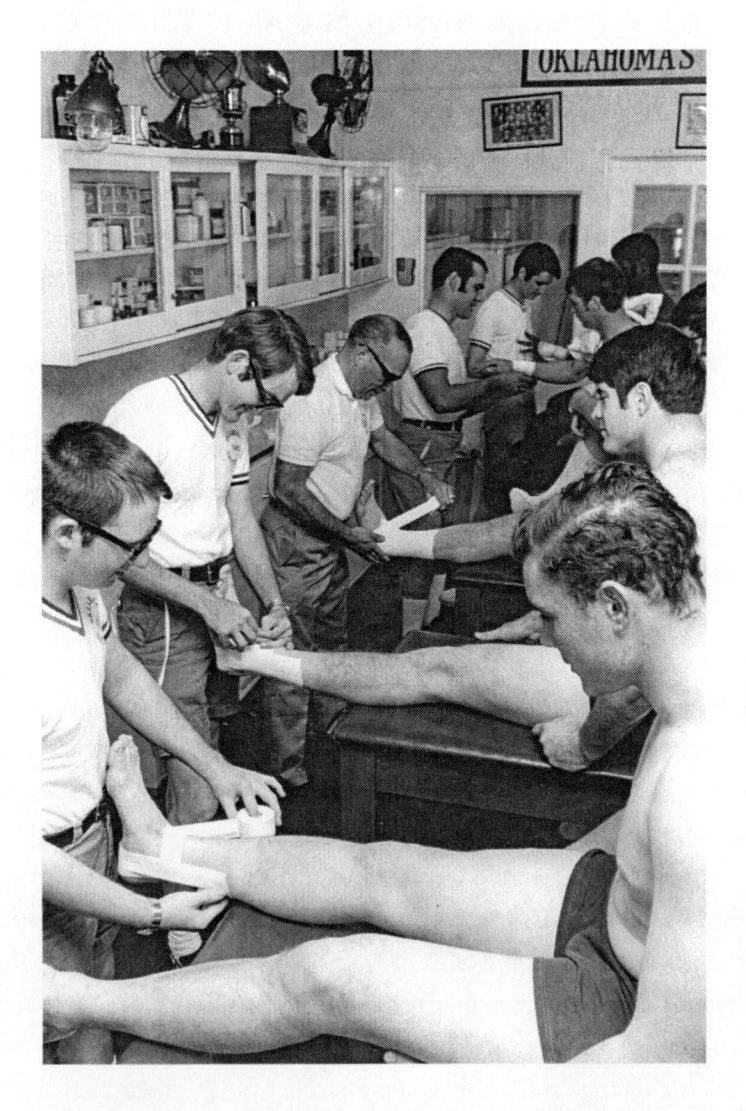

Ken Rawlinson (center) and assistant trainers tape the Sooners before a game.

THE UGH AWARD

BACK TO THE VARSITY YEARS FOR MORE STORIES. HERE ARE A FEW COMMENTS about awards and recognition programs. Sometimes these are suck-up awards or just plain accidents that happened. We had an OU award the coaches made a big deal out of, "The Ugh Award," which was awarded for outstanding defensive play.

The last game of the 1961 season was against in-state rival Oklahoma A&M. Many refer to this university as Oklahoma State. To most of my OU buddies and me, they are still and will always be Oklahoma A&M… the Aggies.

At the beginning of the 1960 season, one of the Phantom and my best friends, the Woodward Flash, Don Derrick, transferred to Oklahoma A&M at Stillwater. As freshmen, the three of us were pretty inseparable. Then, Derrick, the rat fink, transferred to A&M. In spite of it, we still love him…the rat fink. So, fast forward to the final game of the '61 football season—OU vs Oklahoma A&M for the state championship.

Derrick was now the starting tailback for the Aggies and was about all they had on offense. Since Derrick was all they had, the Phantom and I proclaimed the week of the game with OSU, "Get Derrick Week." Game day arrived and the Phantom and his trusty sidekick, the Heavener Flash, just went everywhere Derrick went. Derrick usually had the ball so the Phantom and I looked great on defense that day. We completely ignored our keys and just tried to get Derrick since we had proclaimed it "Get Derrick Week."

Regardless of the fact that he had defected to Oklahoma A&M, Don was a great player. I won the UGH award for Outstanding Defensive play, but only because playing linebacker in the middle of the defensive formation I could go sideline to sideline and the Phantom was stuck on one side of the defense at an end. Half of the UGH Award should have belonged to the Phantom.

OU VS ARMY—YANKEE STADIUM, 1961

IN 1961 THE OU TEAM ALSO HAD A FIRST, WE FLEW TO NEW YORK CITY TO play Army at Yankee stadium. It was the first time OU had played in Yankee Stadium and the first jet airplane ride to a game for the Sooners. Before the game, in our pregame warm ups, I could not get the ball within five yards of our punter, Ronnie Payne. One snap would be five yards to his left...the next one over his head...and the next rolling back on the ground. Finally I looked back and Ron was down in a sprinters stance ready to chase down my snap. It did loosen me up a little as I chuckled out loud at Ronnie's move.

The first time we were on offense and had to punt, I asked our quarterback, Bob Page, on a third down if I could say something in the huddle. He gave me the go ahead. I tried to convey to the team just how very important it was that we pick up the first down. We failed and had to punt.

The anxiety level was off the charts in at least two of the OU Sooners in punt formation...Ronnie Payne and me. I remember praying for a good snap and wondering if there had ever been in recorded history a prayer for divine guidance for a good snap of a football. Some people say they have actually talked to God...well listen up, God did not speak to me but He did sing to me. I will never forget His words. They were...Boomer Sooner, Boomer Sooner, Boomer Sooner, Boomer Sooner, Boomer Sooner, Boomer Sooner, OKU!

A certain serenity engulfed me. My snap was a perfect spiral that drilled through the Yankee Stadium air and hit Ronnie Payne right in the hands. I heard the thud as his foot hit the pigskin and the punt was away. OU scored on a trick play and upset Army. The Sunday New York Times sports headline read, "OU Ambushes Army".

After the game, we were turned loose on New York City. Phil Lohmann, Dennis Ward, and the Heavener Flash all went out together. The first place we went was a bar/night club in Greenwich Village. I had never been in such a place before. I noticed these two ladies over by the bar hugging and kissing each other and these two guys sitting in a booth hugging and kissing each other. So, I turned to this guy I was dancing with and said, "What the hell kind of place am I in here anyway?"

Mike McClellan #31 scored on a center pitchout—the trick play that beat Army.

ALUMNI VARSITY GAME—1963

IT WAS REALLY TOO BAD WHEN THE ALUMNI VARSITY FOOTBALL GAME AT OU became a thing of the past. Let's return to about 1963 for a great story. This story has to be set up, for its basis was a classic Bud Wilkinson pregame story. It came to be known as "The Bird Story." Here it is…

There once was an old philosopher that lived in a village far, far away. The old philosopher was known far and wide as the smartest and wisest in the land. He could answer any question with the right answer. One day a young philosopher moved into the area. Almost immediately he began to hear about the deeds and fame of the old philosopher. The young philosopher came up with a plan to discredit him. It appeared to be a foolproof way, too.

The young philosopher would go to the old philosopher and have a bird in his hand. He would then confront the old philosopher with this question, "Old philosopher, is this bird alive or is it dead?" If the old philosopher said it was alive, then the young philosopher would simply clinch and tighten his grip, killing the bird, and proving the old philosopher wrong. But if the old philosopher said the bird was dead, then the young philosopher would open his hand and the bird would fly away proving the old philosopher wrong. It was a fail proof plan.

So, bird in hand, the young philosopher set out to confront the old philosopher. When he stood face to face with the old philosopher, he asked him, "Is this bird alive or is it dead?" The old philosopher thought for a moment and then said, "As you will, my son…as you will." Bud Wilkinson would then continue, "Men, the outcome of this game today is the same answer…as you will…as you will. It is up to you and your attitude. If you think we will win, then we will. As you will, my son, as you will!"

Now let's fast forward to the OU Spring game versus the old grads in 1963. Frank "Pop" Ivy was the head coach of the Alumni team. The

'63 Varsity team was giving us all we wanted and Pop was trying to fire us up at the halftime. Ed Gray, a tackle of the vaunted OU teams that were early 50s national champions, interrupted Pop with this gem. "Shit, Pop, tell the Bird Story and we will go out there and kick the crap out of them!" It cracked up the locker room.

It was wonderful playing in those games. Spread around the locker room that day were former OU greats Clendon Thomas, Tommy McDonald, Prentice Gautt, Ronnie Payne, Ross Coyle, Karl Milstead, Tom Cox, Dennis Ward, Duane Cook, Leon Cross, Jimmy Harris, and the Heavener Flash himself, Johnny Tatum. And on the defensive team, Jim Weatherall, Billy Pricer, Bobby Boyd, Kurt Burris, Bob Harrison, Mike McClellan, Jerry Thompson, and Don Stiller to name just a few.

Pop's bird story must have worked—the Alumni came back in the second half and won the 1963 game.

Four truly great figures in OU sports history—Leon Cross, Wally Johnson, Jimmy Carpenter, and the best linebacker I ever tried to block, former NFL star Bob Harrison.

> "I feel like I was shot through a forest and hit every tree." sighed Center Johnny Tatum, when interviewed in dressing room after 1964 Varsity-Alumni game, won 16-6 by the 'arsity(only their 4th win in 16 games).
>
> It was Johnny's first football in a year.

First draft of an article in an OU press release after the 1964 Varsity-Alumni game.

NOTABLE OU PLAYERS

THE CHALLENGE OF A CHAPTER ON NOTABLE OU PLAYERS IS HOW DO YOU decide which ones to write about. There are so many to choose from in such a storied program as OU—it could fill a dozen books like this. To keep the list shorter, I will select those individuals that were instrumental to the time period 1958 to 1963…JET's years at OU.

JD ROBERTS

The first person would be J.D. Roberts. JD was known as Jess or JD… Jess was a nickname and JD was an abbreviation for John David. JD played guard for Bud Wilkinson's Sooner teams in the early 1950s and won the Outland Trophy as the nation's best lineman his senior year, 1953. After a stint in the USMC, JD went to work as an assistant coach and after a couple of years, he went to work as a line coach for OU and Gomer Jones, the Offensive and Defensive Line Coach for the Sooners.

In 1958, JD was in charge of recruiting in Southeastern Oklahoma. He called the football coach at McAlester, Oklahoma and asked him if there were any players he should be looking at in Eastern Oklahoma. The coach at McAlester told him about a fullback and linebacker at Heavener, Oklahoma named John E. Tatum—that is how I came to know JD Roberts. He started to recruit me to play football at OU and that would change my life forever. JD Roberts was a godsend to me. It would prove to be a one-way ticket out of poverty and an opportunity of a lifetime as an Oklahoma Sooner football player.

My ability to run fast, tackle, and play football led to the most fantastic opportunity ever for a poor kid from the Ouachita Mountains in Southeastern Oklahoma. The day after I graduated from Heavener High

School, I put all my belongings in a brown paper grocery sack, walked a couple of blocks east to highway 59 and hitchhiked to Oklahoma City. I had five dollars in my pocket, my last paycheck from Hembree Chevrolet, where I worked on Saturdays and a big dream of a better life in Norman, Oklahoma.

I felt as I waited for a ride to carry me from hard times that I was just about the luckiest man alive. For I was on my way to a life filled with promise. And all I had to do to fulfill that promise was go to school, make good grades, and play a game that I not only loved, but would pave the way to opportunity unlimited. The future would prove, too, that all my dreams could come true. All I had to do was to work hard, study, and become disciplined in every way.

When I arrived in Oklahoma City, OU and namely JD Roberts were waiting for me. I stayed with an Aunt and Uncle, Al and Bonnie Robertson. JD had found me a job as a hod carrier working on building what would become Penn Square Shopping Center. I would catch the bus on Western Avenue and ride the bus to and from work. I made more money than I had ever had in my life and saved everything I could. The week before I was to leave for school at OU, my Aunt Bonnie took me to Rothschild's Men's store and picked out some clothes for school, which I paid for.

When I arrived at OU, I had a room in a brand new athletic dormitory, Washington House. It was right across from the southeastern corner of Owen Stadium. I had everything a human could possibly want...a clean room, three nutritious hot meals a day with all you could eat portions, all the books I could read, and an open ended opportunity that afforded me an endless opportunity.

My Aunt Bonnie had sent me a card when I graduated from high school. It was a poem by Rudyard Kipling called, "IF." I have kept that poem, framed and hanging in my home every day since receiving it. The last stanza of the poem is, "And if you can fill the unforgiving moment with 60 seconds worth of distance run, yours is the earth and everything that is in it and which is more, you'll be a man my son." That became and has always been the creed I have tried to live by.

J.D. Roberts, 1953 Outland Trophy winner, with George, the Sooner football team's mascot. George's home was in a dog house outside the athletic dorm. All the team members took care of their mascot, including overfeeding him with food from the training table.

OU Outland Trophy winners, given to the top interior lineman in the nation are Jim Weatherall, 1951; J.D. Roberts, 1953; Lee Roy Selmon, 1975; Greg Roberts, 1978; Jammal Brown, 2004.

Coach Gomer Jones talks to Outland Trophy winner J.D. Roberts, #64

But even though my God had given me enough athletic talent, I knew that it was still up to me to perform and improve every day and fully use whatever talent I had. I knew that somehow I needed to prove JD right in his unyielding belief that despite my size, I could indeed play football at the Division One level.

JD left the OU coaching staff and I felt disconnected. There was no one to champion my cause, so to speak. So, by default almost, Port Robertson became my guiding light. I was like a wild horse spitting out the bit at every turn. But thank God, Port didn't have the word quit in his vocabulary. I did not know it then, but I could not have had a better mentor as Port. More about Port later…

You can see why JD Roberts will always be a shining star in my life and at the top of my list of all great OU football players.

RON PAYNE

Ron Payne was a rugged football player at OU from Breckenridge, Texas. Breckenridge High School turned out many outstanding football players and my good friend and teammate, Ron Payne arguably may have been the cream of the crop! At OU, Payne played both ways, as every player of that era did. Payne was a tight end on offense and an end on defense as well and was also the punter. In sizing up Payne as a college football player, it is my opinion that he was the best player OU had in the 1959-60-61 seasons. In 1961, he led the team in pass receptions.

The 1961 season was unusual in that OU lost the first five games but then won the last five games of the season. And four out of the remaining five games were away...Mizzou, Army, Nebraska, and Kansas. Mizzou was a three or four touchdown favorite. When the '61 OU team defeated Mizzou at Columbia, it began a conference winning streak that propelled OU to a 1962 Big 8 conference championship, Coach Wilkinson's final championship at OU.

The 1961 season came to an end and I would say farewell to several of the best friends I would ever make...Karl Milstead, Tom Cox, Ron Payne, Dale Perini, Billy White, Bob Page, Jimmy Carpenter, Mike McClellan, and Dr. Paul Benien.

The sports media would dub the '61 OU team as the "Come Back Team" of the year. The Sooners of 1961 would go 5-5 but set the stage for a good 1962 team to be Big 8 Champions, a streak started with the 1961 Sooner football team. The '62 team swept the Big 8, winning against each Big 8 team...Iowa State, Kansas, Kansas State, Mizzou, Nebraska, Colorado, and Okie State. Coach Wilkinson would resign as the OU Head Football coach the following year, thus ending one of the great careers in college football.

SOONER FOOTBALL

RON PAYNE—OU END AND CFL STAR DEFENSIVE END

Ron "Catfish" Payne and wife, Becky, at their 50th wedding anniversary. Becky Olive was my lab partner in Human Anatomy and Physiology class at OU. Her parents credit me for getting her through OU. And, I introduced her to Ron Payne—she has never forgiven me for that.

PRENTICE GAUTT & WALLY JOHNSON—TWO HISTORIC SOONERS

Any book with stories about Sooner football, Old School, would be incomplete without the mention of two historic OU players—Prentice Gautt and Wallace Johnson. Prentice and Wally grew up in Oklahoma City not far from each other. Both were star athletes for Oklahoma City Douglas High School. Both were fullbacks and linebackers. Prentice was the oldest by a couple of years. Prentice Gautt became the first African-American athlete at OU and his friend Wallace followed him, becoming the second African-American athlete at OU.

Both Prentice and Wallace were excellent students and great athletes. Prentice excelled at OU and went on to play in the NFL. After football ended for Prentice, he went on to become the Associate Commissioner of the Big 8 Conference. Numerous honors were bestowed on Prentice. He was the "Jackie Robinson" at Oklahoma University and old JET knew Prentice well and called him a great friend. Prentice was a gentleman's gentleman.

I have often wondered if Prentice and Wally knew just how historic they were in OU sports history. Wallace Johnson did not become the star athlete that Prentice was. Fate was not a friend to Wally as a broken ankle and serious knee injury shortened his playing days on the gridiron. Wally nevertheless became a star in the OU ROTC program.

Upon graduating from OU, Wally was commissioned a second lieutenant in the US Army Infantry. He went through several advanced training courses in the Army and in 1966 was assigned to the 10th Special Forces and served 13 months in Vietnam, Laos, and Cambodia, rising to the rank of Captain. He was extracted from SE Asia and spent six months in a military hospital before his next assignment. Wallace ended up as an instructor in modern warfare at Fort Leavenworth, Kansas.

Bill Hill, the Marlow Flash, was stationed at Fort Leavenworth at the same time. One day, not long after Wally had arrived at the base, another officer was talking to Bill and mentioned that he had met a newly assigned officer that, like Bill Hill, was an ex OU athlete. Bill inquired as to the ex OU athlete's name and was told it was Wallace Johnson. Bill flat out denied that there had been any Wallace Johnson playing football in the early 60s. That was when Bill had played there. How dare some guy claim to have played at OU.

So, just to make certain, Bill called the OU athletic department and asked to speak with the guru of OU athletic history, none other than PGR...Port Robertson. Bill said, "Hello Coach, this is Bill Hill at Ft. Leavenworth, Kansas. There is a guy here by the name of Wallace Johnson claiming to have played fullback at OU. Does such a guy exist?"

Port replied, "Hey Bill, how is old Wally doing? Great guy Wallace

Johnson is. Give him my kindest regards." Wild Bill had a plate of crow to eat. After some checking, Wallace was in fact the real McCoy and not only did Wally play at OU and was the second black athlete to break the color barrier, he was also a Lt. Col. in the 10th Special Forces and an expert on guerrilla warfare.

Prentice Gautt and Wallace Johnson are exceptional men. I believe if one were to look up class acts in the dictionary, you would find a picture of Prentice and Wallace—two former Sooners who distinguished themselves in so many ways throughout their lives and were an important part of the great Sooner tradition. Old JET is much richer for having known them both.

Prentice Gautt turns the corner in a Spring Alumni Game with JET (#64) in pursuit.

JET and Lt. Col. Wallace Johnson, US Army (Retired)

JOE DON LOONEY

Old JET had the great pleasure of playing at OU at the same time as two of the most infamous football players in the Bud Wilkinson era. This was a time when the Bud Wilkinson regime was exactly like John Wayne toilet paper, it did not take any crap off of anyone! Those two infamous players were Wahoo McDaniel and Joe Don Looney. I will not address the Wahoo McDaniel legacy as I was only at OU for one of Wahoo's years.

I did have one personal run in with Wahoo. I roomed with upper classman Max Morris from Littlefield, Texas. Our room was three doors down from Wahoo and 1959 Football team captain, Gilmer Lewis. Now there is an enigma for you. G.A. (Gilmer) was one of the nicest players at OU, rooming with arguably the biggest ass hole on the team…Wahoo!

One day I was walking down the hall in Washington House, the brand new athletic dormitory. When passing Wahoo and G.A.'s room I heard

Wahoo yell, "Hey you damn freshman get in here." So, I stopped and went into their room.

Wahoo was sitting on the bottom bunk bed and said, "Hey you damn freshman, see those boots in the closet, I want you to shine them for me."

Without hesitation I looked straight at him and said, "I don't shine shoes for some sorry rude asshole like you!" Wahoo instantly slid off his bed and started toward me with his fist clenched. I knew he was going to try to punch my lights out so I met him in the middle of his room with a right cross punch squarely to his jaw. It did not slow him down and the fight was on.

This was only about the second week that I had been on campus and in the athletic dormitory. As Wahoo came toward me, I could only think about what my good friend from Heavener and Tulsa University football player had told me about the "pecking order" college football teams had. Dave Selph had advised me that the upper classmen would establish such an order at OU, too. And when they did, Dave advised me to fight like a crazy man and when and if I did, the upper classmen would leave me alone.

Wahoo and I did battle for about three furious minutes, after which I was bleeding from about every orifice of my body. But the good news… so was Wahoo. And Dave Selph was right, the word went out, don't mess with the kid from Heavener, for he is truly crazy. And that was the last time Wahoo ever spoke to me.

G.A., however, was extra kind and respectful. He was truly a cool guy and I could see why the OU team elected him the team captain. Gilmer was a tackle and a good one.

It was 1963 and OU opened up with USC. Southern Cal was ranked #2 in the nation with OU ranked #1. The game was played in California at their stadium. OU won the game and Joe Don Looney had a career day. On the next Tuesday at practice, Joe Don was in a snit because he was still on the depth chart as the alternate unit halfback. He was heard to say to many, "What do you have to do around here to be on the starting team?"

The truth was, there was only a little difference between either the starting or alternate unit. Joe Don just enjoyed bitching about the small stuff.

In this accurate account of the Saga of Joe Don, an important fact is, after the victory over USC, OU had an open date before they would play the Texas Longhorns in the Cotton Bowl in the annual Red River Rivalry in Dallas. It was early in the practice that Tuesday in the open date week of the OU schedule. The team had just finished with calisthenics when the different groups went to position drills. I was a graduate assistant and was assigned to a halfback blocking drill run by backfield coach Jay O'Neal. Another grad assistant and I held air dummies and played like defensive ends. Jay O'Neal, standing behind the backs, would motion to us defensive ends and tell us to crash, box, stay, or float, mimicking the moves of real defensive ends. The players in that practice were in full gear.

It was Joe Don's turn and Jay signaled to me as a defensive end to crash down inside. I did, and Joe Don, without his helmet on like everyone else, scraped his ear on the dummy I was holding. Joe Don had some choice words for me and I quickly retorted, "Well Joe Don, if you had your head gear on, you wouldn't have been hurt!" He mumbled something as he turned and walked back and got into line again.

When it was his turn in the drill again, he assumed his stance and this time he had his headgear on. He was now in full gear...shoulder pads, headgear, knee and thigh pads...the whole nine yards. Jay O'Neal signaled for me to stay, which I did. Joe Don came to execute the block. But rather than hitting the air dummy, Joe Don threw a wicked forearm shiver at my face. However, my cat like reflexes kicked in and I shoved the air dummy into Joe Don's face. He then took a wild swing at me and the fight was on.

I was in coaching shorts, a tee shirt, whistle, and tennis shoes...Joe Don was armor plated. I took him down on the ground and struggled to remove his helmet so I could brain the 235-pound prima donna asshole. I finally removed his headgear and drew it back, ready to return the fire to Joe Don when the coaches grabbed me. The fight ended as quickly as it had begun. The only damage Joe Don inflicted on me was a torn tee shirt. And that was it.

Nothing much was ever said about our scuffle. It was not unusual for "fights" to break out during practices. After all, the testosterone levels amongst that group ran at a pretty high level. Besides, in just eleven days the Sooners had to be ready to play Texas.

During those eleven days nothing much was ever said about our fight during practice except for Gomer Jones who constantly kidded me about "picking on Poor Joe Don." Hell, getting teased by Gomer was sort of a compliment anyway. Besides, I loved Gomer and his teasing was his way of saying, "Tatum, you are alright!"

I am not certain about what happened in the Cotton Bowl. I know we lost to Texas. A lot of stories about Joe Don swirled around after the game.

It was the Monday following the loss on Saturday to Texas and I was in a car traveling from Oklahoma City US Grant High School where I was doing my practice teaching. The news broke in over the radio. "Breaking news from the OU football offices, Joe Don Looney has been dismissed from the football team for getting into a fight with assistant football coach, John Tatum."

I was stunned. How could that be? If Joe Don was to be removed from the team, why wasn't it done twelve days ago when he took a swing at me?

I never talked to Coach Wilkinson about the incident and no one associated with the Sooner football program then or at any time since has told me the real story of why I was thrown under the bus, so to speak.

My best guess is this. I believe Joe Don, in the minds of the OU fans, was so good that Bud needed a plausible excuse to kick Joe Don off the team. Fighting with a coach was that defensible reason.

In the final analysis and after much thought, I was ready to fall on the sword for my beloved Sooners, no matter what the reason was. Nothing could trump my gratitude for JD Roberts finding me and giving me a one-way ticket out of Heavener and the bleak future life held for me there. JD Roberts, operating on behalf of OU, was like a guardian angel finding me. So, in the final analysis, the Joe Don incident was just not a big deal, no matter what. For in my mind coming home to OU is a perfect ending to my time on this earth. For I am Sooner reborn and Sooner bred and when I die, I will be Sooner dead.

On the Sunday or Monday following the Texas loss, Coach Wilkinson left it up to the team as to what to do with Joe Don. The team voted to dismiss Joe Don. Exactly what that means, this writer is not certain. So, was it the team, the team captains, or a select group of players that voted to dismiss Looney? Bill Hill, a tough hardnosed tackle from Marlow, Oklahoma and former roommate of Joe Don could not remember having voiced an actual vote, either for the action or against the move to oust his former roommate and teammate.

Bill added this comment as to adding to the reasons to dismiss Joe Don from the team. According to Bill, the Sooner offense was having a great deal of trouble blocking the Texas middle linebacker. That linebacker was Tommy Nobis. The OU coaches concocted a scheme that called for a double team block on Nobis involving Bill Hill and Joe Don. Bill was to hit him and then release, allowing Joe Don to come from the outside and hit Nobis at full speed. And, Looney was a large running back at 6'2" and 235 pounds. However, the scheme did not work and Joe Don got his bell rung by the rugged Texas middle linebacker. Then following that fiasco, according to several OU sources, Joe Don refused to enter the game again.

Following the Texas–OU game, clearly Coach Wilkinson had a real dilemma on his hands. And it was de ja vu all over again with the Great White Father. For in 1957-59, Wilkinson had dealt with a very similar situation with a gifted player named Wahoo McDaniel, a tight end and fullback. And Joe Don reminded Coach Wilkinson of a time gone by that caused the Oklahoma Football program many problems. This time, Coach Wilkinson would intervene and nip it in the bud.

It really does not matter how the story of Joe Don's ending at OU is written. Knowing Coach Wilkinson as a former player and a graduate assistant coach, he was a fair man. My guess is that a series of events all came together and created a huge problem. And that problem caused serious morale problems on the team.

Coach Wilkinson was a very focused CEO type leader. Strong leaders respond quickly to problems that cause negative results. Knowing Coach as well as anyone, my guess is he called together various team leaders one at a time, surveyed their thoughts and feelings about the issue, and when he had a consensus, he acted to eliminate the issue. That is what good leaders do, solve problems, and Joe Don had become a problem to the OU football program. The problem was not just one thing but a collection of things.

Joe Don Looney had come to OU via Cameron Jr. College at Lawton, Oklahoma. After spring football and two a days in August, Joe Don was on the third team. The Sooners opened the 1962 season against the Orangemen of Syracuse University. The story actually began late in the fourth quarter with OU trailing Syracuse 3-0. Syracuse had the football, fourth and one yard with the Orangemen just inside the 30-yard line in OU territory. Syracuse went for it on fourth down. With about three minutes remaining in the game, all Syracuse had to do was make that one yard and they would have either kicked another field goal or scored a TD. The Sooner defense stopped them.

The Sooners took over with about two and a half minutes remaining in the game. After a couple of short gains, over on the OU sideline, the Cameron Juco halfback, #33 Joe Don Looney, approached Coach Wilkinson. He got the Great White Father's attention and said, "Coach, if you want to win this damn game, just put me in and I will win it for you!" Coach Wilkinson did just that.

On the first carry, Joe Don Looney went wide off our offensive left side, split three Orangemen defensive backs, shot up the east boundary on a 70-yard brilliant run—TOUCHDOWN OU. Thanks to Joe Don Looney, OU escaped with a 7-3 victory in what would become one of the all-time best games ever played at Owen Field. It would also become Joe Don's coming out party.

The epilogs on the Saga of Joe Don Looney and Wahoo McDaniel have very similar endings. Wahoo returned to OU and apologized to Port Robertson for all of his shenanigans. Joe Don did the same. Both guys were, down inside, good ole boys with perhaps just a little too much testosterone. But then again, college football is a brutal sport played by very tough hombres. And, when you are 18-21 years old, one is more than just a little likely to have episodes where they can be eaten up with the dumb ass! When you suffer from attacks of the dumb ass, one's decision making makes one's level about a half a bubble off.

Joe Don Looney had several chances to prove Bud Wilkinson wrong in dismissing him from the Sooner football squad. Joe was drafted by the NFL and subsequently played for several different teams. Joe did not last long with any team as he continued to be a problem on and off the field. One team he was traded to was the Baltimore Colts with Don Shula as the head coach. Current Alabama Athletic Director and good friend of old JET shared this story when Nancy Jean and I had dinner with Bill and Mary Battle in Birmingham, Alabama a few years ago. As a member of the Colts team, Joe Don was missing a lot of assignments. This began to bother Shula. Shula had noticed that former Alabama fullback and defensive back Butch Wilson had struck up a friendship with Looney.

Coach Shula asked Butch Wilson to invite Looney to dinner and discuss the importance of executing his assignments. Wilson invited Joe for dinner and when the opportunity presented it, he began to talk to Joe about doing his job because the team was counting on every player to do his part in making the offense click. After about a ten-minute talk about responsibility, Butch asked Looney if he had any questions. Joe Don responded with this gem. He said, "Butch, have you ever noticed all those pigeons that fly around in the stadium?"

Butch acknowledged that he had seen them. Joe Don then asked Butch, "Have you ever wondered where the birds go?" That ended the discussion. Joe was traded to another team. That sort of explains why Joe Don Looney was difficult to deal with. Some players wondered if Joe Don ever really wanted to be a football player or was he just trying to please someone else?

One thing was not up for debate. Joe Don Looney was a very gifted athlete. He could run fast, was football savvy, and was a heck of a punter, too. He was 235 pounds of muscle who could not only run around you but run over you, too.

Johnny Tatum and Joe Don Looney hoist defensive back Wes Skidgel as they get a break from football practice at Miami Beach. The newspaper clipping details the untimely death of Joe Don in a motorcycle accident in west Texas.

Joe Don Looney, #33

LEON CROSS—THE OLD RUGGED CROSS

When Nancy and I moved back to Norman we were excited to be close to the University and so many different sports activities. The move also put me back in touch with a close friend and former teammate, Leon Cross. We called him the "Old Rugged Cross" when we played together. He had been sidelined a couple of different years with terrible knee injuries. Leon actually spent six years at OU as a player due to hardship injuries.

Leon is the consummate OU sports fan. He watches it all and his life is just one big sporting event. He is retired from coaching football at OU and then spending a couple of decades as an Assistant Athletic Director.

Leon knows more people in Oklahoma than anyone I have ever known. It comes from years of recruiting and even more years of raising money for worthwhile OU sports projects. I must say this about Leon, if someone starting ranking those who love OU athletics the most, Leon would certainly end up in the top ten for sure. He bleeds Crimson and Cream.

Without a doubt, Leon is OU's number one men's and women's gymnastics fan. He never misses a meet and often follows the teams on the road to the Nationals. There are none of my friends more knowledgeable about OU sports history than Leon. His recollection of OU trivia goes from the early 50s to the present. He personally recruited many OU legends.

Leon is a confirmed bachelor who has never married. I believe with all my heart he did marry once upon a time. His bride's name…OU. That has been my dear friend Leon's life since he was an 18-year-old freshman from Hobbs, New Mexico at OU. I believe it was love at first sight between Leon and his beloved OU.

It mattered not to him whether he was teaching young men to block and tackle or read keys playing defense. He did not care whether he was off recruiting or trying to raise money for some worthwhile OU project. If the activity involved OU, then Leon was gung-ho to successfully get the job done. He is the kind of guy corporations build great organizations around.

Dedicated, loyal, tireless, focused, and relentless was Leon Cross when it came to the Sooner sports nation. For the well-informed Sooner supporter, you can see Leon Cross's influence everywhere on the Sooner campus. In buildings, arenas, history, players, and traditions, Leon's presence is there. I am fortunate and happy to have such a dear friend. My life has been richer for having had Leon's friendship.

The Old Rugged Cross and JET—Leon was the 1962 football team captain and retired from OU as an Assistant Athletic Director.

BILL WATTS—AKA COWBOY BILL

If you were to poll the sports world and ask, "Who is Bill Watts?" perhaps a small handful of sports fans would remember him as a promising young football player from an Oklahoma City high school, Putnam City High School, and the Oklahoma Times Lineman of the Year in 1957, who, though highly recruited, signed with the OU Sooners under Bud Wilkinson.

But if you changed the question by a few words and asked it like this, "Who is Cowboy Bill Watts?" You would likely have a plethora of professional wrestling fans acknowledge Cowboy Bill as one of the greatest pro wrestling superstars ever. A wrestler known for drawing record crowds in all the top venues in America, as well as the historical ones like Madison Square Garden in New York City, The Cow Palace in San Francisco, the HIC in Honolulu, as well as the Superdome in New Orleans.

He was considered to be one of the top box office attractions, and has been inducted into all three of the Pro-Wrestling Halls of Fame. He was also featured in the Saturday Evening Post in an article written by Myron Cope, entitled: "The Rich, Full Life of a Bad Guy."

This is the same person who came to the Oklahoma Sooner program as a tackle. Bill Watts was only 17 years old when he entered OU as a freshman. And he had not really started to grow and mature…but he did in Norman, and that was his downfall. By the end of his freshman year, Watts was at 245 pounds, but the coaches made him lose to 215, then at 229 his junior year, he was the biggest man on the team, and had a hard time trying to stay at their assigned weight for him. Ken Rawlinson, the OU trainer, put him on what he called the Mayo Clinic diet, which featured eggs, eggs, eggs, and grapefruit. In fact, Watts says, "I ate so many eggs, I thought I was going to grow feathers!" (Later, Watts checked with the Mayo Clinic who denied they ever had such a diet, and that diet would NOT even be good for an athlete!)

He wrestled at OU at 245 pounds, under Port Robertson and Tommy Evans. He relates a funny story about Port, whom we all respected. He said, "Port once told me, that if he was to tell me to 'haul ass' it would take two trips!" Another distinction then, Watts and Stan Abel, another wrestler at OU from Putnam City High School, were the most penalized by Port of all the athletes, and accumulated 10,000 Stadium Steps punishment. We all dreaded that, because you had to make it to the top of Owen Stadium in 15 seconds for it to count. Watts and Abel spent one whole summer running them.

Coaches then had such endearing psychology, because at 245 pounds, Watts definitely was not fat. He was clearly way ahead of his time in the Sooner football program that had a 'built for speed' mentality.

Watts was in a never-ending battle with the Sooner coaches over his size. After a severe 'car-train wreck' his sophomore year, where his diagnosis was critical, then downgraded to he will never walk again, then downgraded to he will never play football again, he came out of the hospital under 200 pounds.

Watts was introduced to weightlifting by Lynn Hickey (who later became known in the Oklahoma City area in the car business), and was a friend and football player from Bethany, who went into the Marines at 138 pounds, and came out at 218 pounds, due to weight training. Seeing that Watts became a proponent of weightlifting, which the Sooner coaching staff opposed, feeling that weights would make their players muscle bound and slow (even though All-American tackle, Jerry Thompson, and guard, Billy Jack Moore, lifted weights all through high school in Ada, OK, the high school team in Oklahoma then that had won more state championships than all the rest. In seven months, Watts went from 245 pounds, to 305 pounds, and was literally 'Superman.'

Watts (who by now also owned a weightlifting gym on campus corner), finally would also show up in the OU wrestling room and deal the varsity wrestlers misery.

Bill Watts just never really fit in the sports culture at OU and that was a terrible outcome for both Bill Watts and OU athletics. Clearly, Bill was just way ahead of his times. His last year in the athletic dorm may have been 1960.

In 1961, Watts signed with the Houston Oilers, in the second year of the AFL, but got into a 'disagreement' with the head coach and was fired.

Bill Watts ran into an old teammate at a bar. Both had been athletes at OU. The ex-Sooner with Watts was none other than Wahoo McDaniel who was playing pro football and then wrestling in the 'off-season.' Wahoo was trying to cash a check so he could buy a round of drinks. He showed the $2500 check to Watts. Wahoo explained to Watts the check was for wrestling. Bill asked if that was for a month. Wahoo said, "No" and Bill asked, "Is it for a week?"

"No, Bill, it was for one night!"

Bill said, "Who do I have to kill, I can beat you in 90 seconds!"

And Wahoo said, "I'll get you started in it." (At this time, Danny Hodge, one of the greatest amateur wrestlers of all times at OU, was wrestling pro, and Dale Lewis, a two time NCAA champ in wrestling at OU was, too.)

Soon after that, Bill Watts headed for Indianapolis and a farm team for the NFL, the Indianapolis Warriors. He also became a professional wrestler and was helped by Dale Lewis, who was wrestling out of that office then.

Bill Watt's weightlifting, which resulted in dramatic size and strength (muscle) was phenomenal then. He wrestled 'pro' for 25 years at 295 to 305 pounds, a long way and dramatic change from the OU coaches reasoning.

He was just a couple of years ahead of his time at OU. In 1965, he bench-pressed 585 pounds. The strongest man in that lift in the world then was Bruno Sammartino, another pro-wrestler; but since both of them were 'pro' those lifts were not recorded. That, too, was another distinction then, lifting records were considered amateur. Neither Watts nor Sammartino ever took a steroid!

In 1962, Eddie McQuarters from Tulsa Booker T. Washington High School joined with one Ralph Neeley from Farmington, New Mexico and the two ushered in the new age of Sooner football, the age of the big fast guys. Eddie played at about 245 and Ralph played at about 260. Dr. Rick McCurdy was a big tight end and Knute Burton was a big guard. A new dawn had risen in the Sooner football camp. New ground had been broken and the Sooners were on their way to NFL sized players.

It was a shame that large athletes like Cowboy Bill Watts had been ahead of their time. Bill Watts, who also built the third largest pro-wrestling TV production and syndication business in America, sold his company in 1987 and retired from professional wrestling. He now resides in a home just 300 yards from the beautiful Gulf of Mexico around the Miramar Beach area of the Florida Panhandle.

Watts still has 'that rebel spirit' but also is now 'a follower of Jesus Christ.' He remains an avid Sooner fan!

This is just one of many stories from Sooner athletics. Sadly, the road to aspiring Sooner athlete dreams are littered with more broken dreams than uncontrolled elation. But young athletes will always follow that dream—regardless of how it turns out.

SOONER FOOTBALL

Bill Watts, Tackle—aka Cowboy Bill Watts, Pro Wrestler

Cowboy Bill Watts and his lady (left) with JET and Wallace Johnson at the annual Spring game party.

THE EXCEPTIONAL FOOTBALL PLAYERS
WE PLAYED AGAINST

WE PLAYED AGAINST SOME EXCEPTIONAL FOOTBALL PLAYERS FROM SOME great football schools in my five years at OU. We played Pitt, Notre Dame, Syracuse, Texas, Northwestern, and, of course, the Big 8 schools. It may surprise you to hear who the very best players were that I played against. It was these guys: Billy Pricer, Jim Weatherall, Ed Gray, Tommy McDonald, Bob Harrison, Kurt Burris, Bob Burris, Clendon Thomas, Jimmy Harris, Jerry Tubbs, Bobby Boyd, Prentice Gautt, and all the guys I played with and practiced against. The OU Alumni game each spring was the toughest competition we would see all year. Of course most of the old grads we played were either in the NFL or the CFL.

Following are just three of the exceptional non-OU players I had the privilege of playing against...

GAYLE SAYERS—KU SENSATION

During the years my teams played at OU, we were fortunate to have played against some of the great football players to have ever played the game. A gifted running back from Omaha, Nebraska was one such player—Gayle Sayers from Kansas University. In 1962, we were preparing to play the Jayhawks on their home turf in Lawrence, Kansas. All week in practice Gomer would work with the defense and every day, several times per practice, he would warn the entire defense about just how fast and quick this one halfback was. Of course he was talking about Mr. Sayers.

Gomer would particularly watch the inside linebackers' reaction to the scout team's guards and how quickly we reacted to the key they gave on each play. Gomer would warn us if we took a wrong step of only a half yard, we would not be able to get to the hole and stop Sayers, he was just that fast. Over and over and over Gomer cautioned us to read the guard and react quickly because of Sayer's speed and quickness. He would say, "You guys have to watch him all the way. You just cannot believe how quick and fast he is." Gomer must have said it 50 times during practice as we prepared to play the Jayhawks.

Saturday came and my team was playing defense. They ran the inside power sweep and Sayers got loose for a touchdown. He ran it right through the hole I was supposed to cover. I ran off the field to Gomer and said, "Coach, I watched him every step of the way and you know what, he is even faster than you said he was." We went on to defeat Sayers and the Kansas Jayhawks 13-7 in a closely contested football game.

The game was memorable for me for three reasons. First, I played against two really great football players that Saturday from KU. They were Gayle Sayers and another running back, Curtis McClinton, who was maybe the most underrated back in the nation. Curtis was also a track guy. I saw him win the Big 8 high hurdles at Norman one year. The second reason the KU game was so memorable, I made the only bad snap of my career, on an extra point. I snapped the ball a little high but way to hard. Our quarterback, Monte Deere, couldn't handle it, but it was clearly my fault. The play made the score 13-7.

I knew if KU scored again, they would kick the extra point and we would lose by a single point. The loss would pretty much be my fault. I was relieved that we kept KU out of the end zone the rest of the game.

The final reason this game was so memorable, my best boyhood friend, Bob Babcock, was there watching us try to contain the great one, Gayle Sayers. I asked Bob to reflect on that game. Here are his memories, "Since I met John Tatum when he moved in across the street from me when I was five and he was seven years old, we have been great friends. Growing up, we played together constantly—mostly Army during our early years until we learned about girls and football as we got older. I was an avid OU fan even before John was. I still hate Notre Dame for ending our 47 game winning streak.

"I was thrilled when John got his scholarship to OU. The first time I got to see him play was the 1961 OU-KU game in Lawrence, Kansas. My best memory is after the game was over. I ran out onto the field to greet John after the great win. He asked me to go into the Sooner dressing room with him and he would introduce me to Bud Wilkinson. As we walked off the field, I reached down and jerked his chinstrap off his helmet—I wanted it as a souvenir. In the dressing room, I shook hands with Bud Wilkinson, was too awe-struck to remember anything other than that, and happily headed for home with a memory that I'll never forget.

"The following week, I got one of the infrequent letters that John wrote me. He asked if I'd stolen his chinstrap. He went on to tell me that when he went to check out another chinstrap before practice on Monday, Port asked him why he'd lost it. Without an acceptable excuse, Port told him that chinstraps are expensive and he would pay for it with a series of trips running up and down the stadium steps of Owen Field. In a return letter, I did confess, but John had long since paid his dues to Port by running the steps of Owen Field."

JIM NANCE AND JOHN MACKEY—SYRACUSE

Expanding on the Syracuse game story that was Joe Don Looney's introduction to OU football, there were two Syracuse players of note on the field that day. Syracuse led 3-0 with just under three minutes to play. They had the football, fourth and one on about our own 30-yard line. They went for it and ran their star fullback off tackle to our defensive right side. Their fullback was a 230-pound bear like fellow named Jim Nance. Nance went on to become the all time leading rusher in the old American Football League for New England.

I was in the game with my alternate starting unit at my position of strong side linebacker, on the defensive left side. I saw the play and my recognition was quick and decisive. I scrapped off to my right and met Nance squarely in the off tackle hole on my defensive right side. I stood Nance up, but he outweighed me by a good thirty or more pounds. Our defensive back, Paul Lea from Terrell, Texas, came up with his blazing speed and hit Nance high, driving him back and stopping him for no gain. The Sooners took over on downs. We were 70 yards away from a TD and victory. We ran a couple of plays and gained a few yards.

Little did we know something of huge historical significance was occurring on the OU sideline. As described earlier, that is when Joe Don Looney, a junior college transfer from Cameron Junior College, walked up to Coach Wilkinson and said to him, "Coach, if you want to win this damn game, put me in and I will win it for you!" Using his great instinct, Coach Wilkinson sent him in.

Our quarterback called his play, a power sweep off tackle on our offensive left side. Joe Don broke off tackle, disappeared in a cluster of Syracuse defensive backs and then exploded into the open and ran the 70 yards for a TD. We successfully kicked the extra point then held on and won the game 7-3.

Syracuse had another great player in the game besides Jim Nance. He was future NFL Hall of Fame tight end, John Mackey. I doubt that John Mackey will ever read this book but if he does, here is a revelation for him.

OU had an end that played across from John Mackey that day. Our end was a raw-boned kid from Washington DC named John Flynn. John is without a doubt the toughest football player I ever played with at OU. He gave the future NFL star for the Baltimore Colts all he wanted in Norman that afternoon and more. I loved playing linebacker on the left side with John Flynn at defensive end…I could always depend on John to turn back inside all runners where I would be waiting to welcome them to OU defensive football. Not only was Flynn a great defensive end but in addition he may have been the most colorful character during the five years old JET was at OU. Flynn was truly an unforgettable character.

SURPRISINGLY GREAT PLAYERS…

There were a few players we faced that qualified for the "hey you have to be kidding me" category. They became stars in the NFL. The most unbelievable player to earn this honor was Nick Bouniconti of Notre Dame. Nick was hands down the best offensive guard old JET ever played against.

During the game between Notre Dame and OU, played in South Bend under the touchdown Jesus, Nick gave me a lesson in how a guard can block a linebacker. Let me count the ways…he trapped me, he blocked me in and out, doubled teamed me, and isolated me. I was totally confused as to what Nick would do to me next. In all of my days, junior high, high school, and college, never had I played against an offensive lineman as great as Nick Bouniconti.

And now for the great surprise. Nick was drafted by the Miami Dolphins, to play middle linebacker! I could not believe it…the greatest offensive lineman ever, in old JET's humble opinion, to play middle linebacker! This just goes to prove how little I knew about the great one from Notre Dame.

Nick Bounticonti was truly a great offensive guard, but he was even better at middle linebacker. He was in an all pro and after a stellar career was elected to the NFL Hall of Fame. Nick was truly one of the great all time players I ever faced.

Joining Nick in this category was John Mackey from Syracuse University. John Mackey gets into this category most probably because when the Sooners played the Orangemen from Syracuse, John Mackey just had a really bad day. Without a doubt, his bad day was catalyzed by another truly great player, John Flynn.

John played defensive end right across from John Mackey. During the Sooners opening game of the 1962 season, John Flynn had his coming out party. The piece of cake at the party was John Mackey. Flynn absolutely tore Mackey a new one. Because of those memories about my friend John Flynn's dominance of Mackey, I was shocked and astounded at John Mackey's performance as an NFL standout at tight end for the Baltimore Colts. Mackey was perhaps the greatest tight end ever to play the game. But that was not the case in Norman the day he met John

Flynn, just maybe the best defensive end I played with or against. John Mackey went on to become an All Pro tight end and ultimately would be in the NFL Hall of Fame.

1963 ORANGE BOWL AGAINST ALABAMA

OU won the Big 8 championship in 1962 and the right to play Bear Bryant's Alabama Crimson Tide in the Orange Bowl. There were more than a couple of highlights at the Orange Bowl. First of all, the President of the United States was a big buddy of our coach, Bud Wilkinson. President John F. Kennedy had appointed Coach Wilkinson the first ever National Physical Fitness advisor. President Kennedy visited our dressing room prior to the game. I stood about five feet away from him. I was taken aback by how small a man he was. Of course average men look small in a room full of OU football players dressed out in full gear.

Alabama won the game played in the Orange bowl by an embarrassing score of 17-0. I did not play. I was recovering from the fourth knee surgery of my career at OU. It would not have mattered had I played as Alabama screwed us like a tied up dog. They had this thing called a forward pass. We had never seen one before. We kept saying, "Run you cowards, Run." But they kept on throwing those passes.

And oh yeah, they had this guy called Broadway Joe Namath throwing them. And they had a future NFL Dallas Cowboy star named Leroy Jordan who forced four OU fumbles that day. It was really a memorable game because one of their players would come to OU the next fall as a grad assistant. His name—Bill Battle, and he played end for the Crimson Tide. Bill and I became great friends and communicate even to this day. Bill is the current Athletic Director at the University of Alabama.

Perhaps the most memorable thing about the '63 Orange Bowl is not memorable at all to me, which is too bad. I wish it was memorable. The day after the Orange Bowl game, the Miami Rod and Gun Club hosted a deep-sea fishing contest for the players from both OU and Alabama.

Those participants were to meet at 6am in the lobby of the hotel to depart for the fishing tournament.

I was just coming in from a night of drinking and celebrating that I would not have to endure any more two a days, taping sessions with the witch doctor, endure painful injuries, or get my clock cleaned by big mean tough evil football players ever again. It was 6am, and I was three sheets to the wind.

One of my teammates saw me in the lobby and said, "Johnny, are you going fishing?"

In a stupor I said, "Sure, when do we leave?" And I got on the bus, kept drinking beer, and did not remember a thing about going fishing that day. I was, as the saying of the time went, shit faced drunk. So, off I went on a fishing trip I could not ever remember.

About two months later, back in Norman, I got a package in the mail from the Miami Rod and Gun Club, a trophy. Apparently I caught the third largest fish, a Bonita, in the tournament. Sadly, I do not remember a thing about it. I proudly display the trophy in my trophy case. I call it the mystery fish I once caught in the Atlantic Ocean. And if that fish had kept his mouth shut, he would not have been caught!

1950S VS TODAY'S FOOTBALL

TODAY I RUN INTO MANY OU FANS WHO WANT TO COMPARE THE PLAYERS of my era with the ones now. It is impossible to make that comparison because the game is so different. In the old days, the greatest difference was we all had to play both ways and on the kick off and punt teams as well. And this factor made a huge difference in just who could play. I have talked to former OU coaches like Jay O'Neill and Joe Rector and Leon Cross. All of them confirm this fact. OU recruited players in the old days who they figured could play good defense first. Second, they recruited players who had good special teams skills—punters, kickoff, field goal kickers, etc. Then they looked for those with offensive skills last. But no matter which category, you must have possessed great speed and quickness.

To describe the difference between the fifties and football now, let's just take centers. In the old days, centers played all four downs on offense. Centers run blocked. Centers pass blocked. Centers snapped the ball no matter what the formation...T formation with the quarterback under center or single wing with the QB five yards deep. The centers snapped all field goals and extra points. And the centers were the deep snappers on punts, too. Centers did it all.

Now let's look at modern centers. They play three downs and they are out. There is a center for punts and a different center, perhaps, for extra points and field goals. And of course a center that plays the first three downs of a drive. That center goes out when it is time for the kicking game. There is a huge difference in the centers in the old days and the ones now.

I happen to believe, since I was a real center, that we old guys were more versatile at least. Football played with unlimited substitution makes for a much better game. A team like OU travels with probably 60 players. And I would bet they use at least 50 of them in a game. When our generation played, maybe no more than 22 players would play in a game. If the game was a blowout, the third team would get to play. That meant 33 players would play.

I believe because the game had limited substitution, there were more injuries as well. Most of my teammates suffered some sort of severe injury over the course of three years of eligibility. The long and short of it, I would have loved to have played only on one side of the ball, and it would have been on defense. I am convinced I would not have suffered so many injuries that required major surgery to repair had I played one way.

But that was not the way it was. We were warriors. We attacked and we defended, too. We all knew offensive, defensive, and special team's strategy.

Finally, our old guys generation also had to learn considerably more pertinent information than today's modern college football player. There were offensive and defensive scouting reports, kicking game information, our offensive and defensive game plans, and special team's data, too.

So, I also believe we were smarter football players than the players today. But that is just my opinion, and I could be wrong.

JOHN TATUM

John Porterfield blocking for OU fullback Jim Grisham

The same John Porterfield, closing in on Iowa State quarterback—
classic two-way football at OU

Johnny Tatum—an Old School center/linebacker, playing at 188 pounds. Totally a different game in the 1950s from today.

THE DANGER OF PUNT RETURN PRACTICE

ONE DAY, A TUESDAY IN 1962, DURING THE SEASON, AT THE END OF PRACtice, Coach Wilkinson called the team together and announced instead of closing practice with the usual wind sprints, we would end practice by covering punts. The past Saturday in a game, our opponent ran a punt back for a touchdown. The two alternate starting units, along with the third team, would cover punts, rotating one team after another. The freshman teams would return the punts and the deep backs on the freshman punt return teams were not allowed to use a fair catch. The coaches wanted to see the coverage, complete with live tackles. My alternate starting unit was up and Gary Taylor boomed a high deep punt toward the deep back of the freshman team, quarterback Norman Smith from Monahans, Texas.

Just as he caught the ball, he was hit high on the left side by Ralph Neeley, a giant tackle from Farmington, New Mexico and future Dallas Cowboys star. Almost simultaneously, Eddie McQuarters, our guard and future NFL star from Tulsa Booker T. Washington hit Smith low and on the right side. Now to mop up on the freshman QB, center Johnny Tatum hit Smith in the numbers and chin. Smith crumbled to the ground, out cold. The hit on Smith tore up one of his knees, separated a shoulder, and he suffered a nasty gash to his forehead. Neeley weighed about 245, McQuarters tipped the scales at about 235, and Tatum was the smallest at 202—a collective force of 682 pounds. It was a wonder that more damage was not inflicted on the small frosh QB.

Football at this level really is a brutal game. And the most remarkable part of this true story…Norman Smith did not quit, and he ended up as the starting QB his senior year at OU, proving to all that he was truly one tough cookie.

Norman Smith—QB—recipient of the three-man hit on him as a punt returner—
McQuarters, Neeley, Tatum hit…

Eddie McQuarters #64 Guard

OU COACHES WHO WILL ALWAYS BE IMPORTANT TO ME

BOB WARD—TOUGHER THAN A TWO-DOLLAR STEAK

In 1960, the very bottom fell out of the Sooner football program. The Sooners of '60 went 3-6-1. It would be The Great White Father's only losing season. Coach Wilkinson took many steps to correct the disaster that had befallen the mighty Sooners. One noteworthy move was to hire a line coach by the name of Bob Ward. Bob was a small but lethal man who had played for the Maryland Terrapins and had been an All American guard.

Bob had been a paratrooper in the Army and was a really bad actor. He believed in hardnosed football and demanded physical toughness from his players. At every practice, Ward became a stark raving maniac with a whistle. He would get in your face and slobber all over you. He would choke you as he screamed and yelled.

At the beginning of every practice was position drills. Those drills were done to reinforce the basic fundamentals of the game of football. When calisthenics were over, the team would circle around The Great White Father and he would announce the players who were with the position coach for drills. It was during this part of practice that many Sooner linemen became deeply religious. Players would simply bow their heads and pray they were not in Bob Ward's drill group.

It seemed as though Ward would pick out a player for that day and ride him like a horse. Ward would be relentless. One of his favorite players to ride was Karl Milstead, a kick your ass rough tough guard from Athens, Texas. Karl was the target of Bob Ward's ire more so than almost any other Sooner lineman. But Bob Ward did not play favorites. Everyone was the victim of Ward's ire. He just wanted us to play good football and was relentless in that pursuit. I thought Ward hated me and that is why he stayed on my ass.

One day it was my turn in the barrel. We were doing a two man sled drill we called the "Hit, Hit, Hit" drill. Each player would hit the sled three times, then do a seat roll out and come up, taking on players with the right shoulder then the left shoulder. It was a contact drill that stressed good balance. Ward made me repeat the drill about three times then he told me, "Tatum, get back down there and when you roll out, I am going to put you on your ass." Well now, this was the opportunity I had been waiting for...I would knock the Maryland smartass into next week.

I hit the sled...boom boom boom...did a seat roll and launched a forearm shiver from the top of my shoe laces right for old Bob's nose. He stepped to the side and I went flying through the air. I bounced on the ground like an airplane with a pilot who had just completed his first solo landing. I had not quit bouncing when I felt Bob Ward's hands around my throat, choking me and yelling, "See Tatum, you have no balance. How are you going to make tackles when your feet are not under you?" I would not forget this message. Bob Ward was right...doggone it. I did not have good balance, but after that day, my balance got a whole lot better.

Several years later I found Bob Ward's address in an O Club publication. I sent Bob a Christmas card and received back a real nice letter from Bob telling me how I was one of his favorite football players at OU. Gee, I wonder what he would have been like had he not liked me. I miss Bob. In retrospect, I respected him for always telling it like it really was and expecting the very best from our performance in practice and on the playing field. He was tougher than a two-dollar steak and he expected an all-out effort from his charges. No wonder...he was Airborne Infantry in the US Army. Anyone who was willing to jump out of a perfectly good airplane is at least one or two bricks short of a full load.

Bob eventually left OU to become a defensive coordinator. He coached at West Point for a while. I always thought West Point would have been the ideal place for Bob. The discipline and no nonsense attitude was perfect for Bob Ward. He later became the Head Football Coach at his alma mater, Maryland. His players, in a protest against his brutal ways and no nonsense rock'em sock'em football style, refused to report for spring practice. That would spell doom for Bob and his tough ways. As tough as Ward was, it never dawned upon any of us OU players to boycott practice…that would have been unthinkable.

The Sooners of 1961 would go 5 and 5 but set the stage for a good 1962 team to be Big 8 Champions, The Great White Father's last Championship team. A streak started with the 1961 Sooner football team. They finished the season with wins over Mizzou, Nebraska, Kansas State, and Oklahoma State. Then the '62 team swept the Big 8, winning against each Big 8 team…Iowa State, Kansas, Kansas State, Mizzou, Nebraska, Colorado, and Okie State. Coach Wilkinson would resign as the OU Head Football coach the following year, thus ending one of the great careers in college football.

OU eager to start comeback—Tatum, Cox, Milstead, Cross, Payne, and Benien

The Oklahoma University Sooners 1961 Offensive Line

1961 Offensive Line—L-R—Dale Perini, RE; Leon Cross, RT; Karl Milstead, RG; Johnny Tatum, C; Tom Cox, LG (hidden from view); Billy White, LT; Ron Payne, LE

1961 Offensive Line—same guys, at 2014 Spring Practice Game—L-R—Dale Perini, RE; Leon Cross, RT; Karl Milstead, RG: Johnny Tatum, C; Tom Cox, LG; Billy White, LT; Ron Payne, LE

GOMER JONES—THE GREAT WHITE FATHER'S ACE IN THE HOLE

GOMER T. JONES WAS BUD WILKINSON'S SECRET WEAPON. GOMER WAS PERhaps the greatest offensive and defensive line coach who ever coached the game of football. At OU in the late fifties, each recruiting class would be about 50 players, made up of the best football players in Oklahoma, Texas, and New Mexico. And let me make a footnote here about Texas turning out all the great OU football players. This is a fact—OU has had five Heisman Trophy winners. Billy Sims is from Hooks, Texas. Billy Vessels, Steve Owens, Jason White, and Sam Bradford all are from Oklahoma.

Back to Gomer Jones. Gomer is an Honorary Okie because he came to Oklahoma with Bud Wilkinson. Gomer went to school in Big Ten country…Ohio State. He was a lineman for the Buckeyes.

Gomer was a short guy…maybe 5'7" and a bit portly. I loved Gomer. Like most other OU linemen, I played my butt off for Gomer. Gomer was a teacher of basic fundamental line skills at OU. He coached some of the greatest ever linemen at OU. Every practice started with fundamental drills to reinforce basic line skills. In every practice, both spring and fall, we did drills to begin each session. I believe the OU line was the best-coached fundamental team in college football—all because of one man, Gomer Jones.

I recall a story. I had quit coaching and had gone into the insurance business in Durant, Oklahoma. One day I was driving by the Durant High School football practice and stopped and walked down behind the offense, engaged in an intra-squad scrimmage. I knew the head football coach, Bill McCarson, and asked him if it would be okay for me to watch a while. He nodded okay.

As I watched alongside the coaches, the offense ran a fullback dive play off the right guard. The defensive player over the guard, just shading his outside, almost killed the fullback. The Durant line coach chastised the offensive right guard far failing to block his opponent. The offense huddled again and the coach said, "Run the same play." The result was the same. The defensive tackle smashed the fullback for a two-yard loss. The line coach went ballistic. He kicked the right guard off the starting team, saying he was a coward and did not have the guts to block the defender. I had been watching the offensive guard on both plays and saw what the problem was—he had stepped off with the improper foot. His failure to execute the proper fundamental caused him to fail in his attempt to execute the block. It was a simple fundamental error. The real error made on the field was the line coach who did not see the mistake and correct the guard's technique. I am confident with the original guard's size and athleticism, had he stepped with the proper foot, he would have successfully executed the block. I left practice thinking how lucky I had been to have had a guru like Gomer Jones teach me so very much about fundamental offensive and defensive line play.

In 1961, during spring practice, the OU coaching staff moved me back to center and inside linebacker. Those were my natural positions. Gomer was a stickler for linebackers executing the basic fundamentals of a linebacker. It all began with keying the guard. Gomer taught us that when we looked into the backfield, we would be deceived and sent in the wrong direction. After all, one of the purposes of offensive strategy was to deceive or fake out the defenders. Gomer taught us that a guard seldom, if ever, deceives you. In fact, the guard's first step will take you straight to the offensive point of attack. I would sometimes wake up in the night hearing Gomer's voice yelling at me, "Key the guard, Tatum, key the guard."

In high school my speed and reaction time was so much better than most of the players I played against, I could get away with instinct type linebacker play. But at division one college level football, I would not stand a chance to recover from wrong steps and close on the ball carrier. It was imperative I key the guard accurately and make the correct first step in my read of the offensive play.

About halfway through the '61 season we went to Columbia and played the Tigers of Mizzou. They had a great football team coached by the legendary Dan Devine and were heavy favorites to beat us. We ended up winning a hard fought battle, 7-0. On the airplane ride back home to Norman, Gomer was walking down the aisle of the airplane, stopped at my seat and said, "Son, you played a great game today." I thanked Gomer and told him, "Coach, I can hardly wait for you to see the game film. I want you to know that I keyed the guard on every single play today. And do you know what?"

Gomer shrugged, "What?"

I then came forth with this unforgettable jewel, "That keying the guard idea really works!"

Gomer looked at me and said, "No Shit." I felt like a complete idiot. But the simple fact really was, I had mastered the single most important fundamental of successful inside linebacker play…keying the guard.

I went in to see Gomer when I was a few days away from graduation. I thanked him for all the wonderful lessons he had taught me. I thanked him for having become my friend and mentor. Then I asked him if he had any advice for me.

Gomer said, "You are going to coach football aren't you, Johnny?" I told him yes. He then said this to me, "Go somewhere where they have never had a winning program and coach there. There will only be one way to go…up. Never follow a winner, Johnny. There will be only one expectation and that is you must win bigger than the guy before you. And usually you will only look bad. Never follow a winner."

Two years later, Gomer would break his own advice and follow the greatest coach who had ever lived…the Great White Father, Bud Wilkinson. Gomer would be fired two years later. It would be a sad day for me. Gomer was a man I admired and loved.

When Gomer Jones was fired, I was coaching at Oklahoma City Star Spencer. The day after the news of Gomer's firing hit the news, I drove to Norman to see him. I expressed my profound sorrow that he had been dismissed. I will never forget Gomer's response. "Johnny," he said, "If you are a coach and you have never been fired, then you just have not been a coach very long!" Gomer became the Athletic Director at OU and then suffered a massive fatal heart attack only a couple of years later. His funeral was in Norman with many of his former linemen in attendance. It was a sad day for sure, like a close member of your family had passed away.

My close friend and teammate, Leon Cross, a line coach and later an Associate Athletic Director at OU shared this about the selection of Gomer Jones to succeed Bud Wilkinson as the OU Head Football Coach.

"Gomer really did not want to be the Head Football coach," Cross said. "Gomer wanted either backfield coach Jay O'Neal or Bobby Drake Kieth to succeed Bud." Cross went on to explain, "The Board of Regents felt both O'Neal and Kieth were too young to handle the job, so Gomer accepted the job with the idea that he would take it for a few years, let both Jay and Bobby Drake get a few more years of experience, then he would retire and one of those two would take over." It seemed like a good plan but the OU fans were behind the team—Win or Tie! Gomer's tenure at the helm was fraught with peril.

Charley Mayhue, a tough sure tackler who played in the OU secondary was a senior Gomer's first year as head coach. Charley was part of a collection of players for OU that clearly were the most talented in the decade of the 60s. Besides Mayhue there were Glen Condren, Knute Burton, Ralph Neeley, Ed McQuarters, Rick McCurdy, John Garrett, Ron Harmon, Wes Skidgel, Norman Smith, Lance Rentzel, Butch Metcalf, Carl McAdams, Rodney Crosswhite, Ray Hanes, Mike Ringer, Ed Hall, Allen Bumgartner, and Ben Hart. All of these guys were very talented football players.

The 1964 Sooners record was 6-4-1 with losses to USC, Texas, Kansas, and Florida State. They managed to tie Mizzou, 14-14. That was Gomer Jones first season as the OU head football coach and it was his best season. The '65 season was a disaster as the Sooners went 3-7 and became Gomer Jones' Waterloo. Gomer was fired as head coach and become the OU athletic director. Jim McKenzie, from the Arkansas football program, succeeded Gomer as the OU head football coach.

Gomer made one critical mistake. He followed the winningest college football coach in America and had but one way to go…that was a one way ticket to failure. The football coaching staff could not find effective ways to lead the talent that Gomer had inherited. And the players could not find effective leaders among their ranks. It was to become a lethal combination that the man so many of us loved could not handle. His coaching staff had many OU former football players on it. I asked Gomer why he kept so many former players as assistants. He replied, "Johnny, they were the ones that got me to where I was. Had I fired them, I would have felt like the asshole of the year!"

That was Gomer—his loyalty to his assistant coaches became his downfall. He chose to fall on the sword rather than fire the player/coaches he loved. His reluctance to be a head coach was right on. Perhaps he just was not gifted with enough talent and charisma to be a head football coach. For certain he was no Bud Wilkinson, but no one could ever surpass his talents and record as a line coach.

Gomer Jones with All-American Center/Linebacker Bob Harrison

PORT ROBERTSON—MR. DISCIPLINE AT OU

WILL ROGERS IS FAMOUS FOR HAVING SAID, "I NEVER MET A MAN I DIDN'T like." Well, I never met a man I disliked as much as I disliked Port G. Robertson. Port was the head freshman football coach at OU. He was also the head wrestling coach among all the rest of his duties.

In a phrase, behind the scene, Port Robertson was the key man to all OU athletics. To say Port was strict, unyielding, tough, overbearing, disciplined, driving, and overly principled would just not being doing the description of him justice. Frankly stated, I have never in my life met anyone even remotely like Port. The very best thing I have ever heard said about Port is, "He is the type of man I aspire to become someday."

Port was a wrestler at OU then went to the Army and was trained as a field artillery officer. He was a forward observer and directed gunfire on enemy positions in WWII. More about this part of his life later.

After the war, Port returned to OU and eventually became the head wrestling coach. He ran a stellar program but that is not what I want to tell you about. I want to share with you the incredible story of Port Robertson, which has never really been told.

I first met Port in the late summer of 1959. I was an incoming freshman football player on a full athletic scholarship with OU. In our first meeting with Port we were told there was but one way to do things at OU if you were an athlete, Port's way. In no uncertain words we were told if we did not obey Port's rules, we would get a one way ticket back to Podunk or wherever it was we had come from. Essentially Port said, "My way or the highway."

This may sound pretty hard line, and it was. But Port knew something about incoming freshman...they were just plain undisciplined. Port coached something far more important than a sport. Port was the head self-discipline coach. He was the very best one who has ever lived... bar none!

Earlier in the book I told you about my first encounter with Port and his discipline—after the ticket-scalping incident in Dallas at the OU-Texas Red River Shoot-Out game. That was just the beginning of my relationship with Port. He was like a big diaper—always on my ass. I stayed in trouble. I wore a path up and down the Owen stadium Section 5 bleachers. I don't think I missed a day of running stadium steps my freshman year. I had no place to go. I could not quit.

My mother had remarried right before my senior year at Heavener High School. Without going into the details, I will just say I did not get along with my new stepfather. I graduated from Heavener High School on a Friday evening and on Saturday morning, I arose, put all of my belongings in a brown paper grocery bag, walked down to Highway 59, and hitch-hiked to Oklahoma City where I had a job as a construction worker building what is now Penn Square Shopping center.

I saved enough money that summer to buy some clothes for college and put the rest in the bank. I budgeted myself 25 dollars a month spending money. I would never live at home again, and I rarely returned to Heavener. No matter how tough things got for me at OU, I had no place to go. OU was a Godsend for me for at 18 years of age. I was totally on my own. My great-aunt and uncle put me up for the summer. They were a Godsend, too. And Port and his discipline turned out to be another Godsend.

Every four weeks Port would have every student athlete take a grade card to each of your professors. They would indicate how many times you had cut class and what your current grade was. You turned the card back into Port when completed. He gave everyone one week to complete the grade card sheet.

Under Port's system, for every unexcused class cut it was 25 stadium steps. And if you had any grade below a C in any class, you went to study hall three nights a week until the next grade card sheet went out. At study hall, tutors were available in math, English, history, and other subjects. During a school year there were three breaks—Christmas, Spring, and Summer. A grade sheet went out before Christmas break and Spring break. If you had any grade below a C, you stayed in Norman the entire week and went to study hall six days a week for eight hours a day. If you were ineligible in the summer…you went to summer school.

I hated Port's strict regimentation of everything. Heck, POW's had more freedom than we had as OU athletes. Lots of guys couldn't take it and many of them just quit. I suppose for many it was a shock going from being the Big Man on Campus to a sweat hog in Port's Navy. Hardly any of us realized it at the time, but Port was giving us exactly what we needed the most—remedial discipline 101. In Port's system, no one got a free pass. It mattered not who you were or what your credentials in high school were…everyone marched to Port's drumbeat.

Port called us pea heads or little dogs. He would talk to us in ways impossible to not understand. Like, if he wanted to see you in his office at 3pm, he would say, "Now Mr. Tatum, three o'clock is when the little hand of the clock is on three and the big one is on 12… understand?"

We had a player from Amarillo named Billy White who could exactly mimic Port. One day Billy called teammate Ronnie Payne and did his Port imitation. He told Ronnie he wanted to see him in his office and he was already late for the meeting. Payne hotfooted it right over to Port's office. There he stood in Port's doorway. Port looked up and said, "What do you want, Mr. Payne?"

Ronnie responded, "You wanted to see me."

Port said, "Well no, but since you are here get your little butt in here and tell me about the C you are making in Business Management." Port then commenced to chew Payne out.

The next day, Ronnie found out it was actually Billy White who had called, not Port. A few days later, Payne actually got a call from Port. Port started out by saying, "Mr. Payne, you little pea head." To which Ronnie replied, "Oh go to hell, Whitey Boy."

Port said, "Hold on, Ronnie. There seems to be trouble with this line.

Now what was that again?" Payne hung up and ran over to Port's office, hat in hand.

One year it was time for Christmas break. Study hall convened for those failing a subject. A star halfback was supposed to be in study hall. After only one or two interrogations, Port learned the halfback had caught a bus and was heading back home to New Mexico for Christmas. Port reported the AWOL player to Coach Wilkinson who immediately called the parents of the player. The parents met their son at the bus station and handed him a ticket back to Norman on a bus leaving in twenty minutes.

The young OU player was in study hall the next morning after having ridden a bus for almost 20 hours, and the young halfback was back in Port's study hall the next morning. It did not matter who you were…this young halfback was future All American and future NFL Hall of Fame receiver Tommy McDonald.

When team discipline is truly for everyone and no one is spared, then players quickly get the message. Discipline is administered equally and expectations are for fair treatment for one and all. With Port at the helm, and everyone in his navy, the choices were quite simple—adhere to the rules or quit. And many did chose the easy path and quit.

Not so long ago, some of our OU vintage gathered in the Loyd Noble parking lot before a Sooner home football game. Marshall York, team captain of the '60 Sooners, supplied the motor home. Teammates Gary Taylor, Bob Schoal, Leon Cross, and yours truly, John Tatum were there. Bob Schoal was a center and linebacker who had been recruited in about 1957 or so. Bob had become disenchanted and let his emotions get the best of him and decided to quit the team. He told us it was the greatest single mistake he had ever made in his life. And he lamented over how many times he had wished he could undo that decision.

Not many people who have not been there can appreciate just how difficult it was for an incoming freshman to adjust to the OU system that Bud and Port had established. Give Port the credit due him; he did get that one right. Incoming freshmen do not know much and they need plenty of direction.

Discipline was right down Port's alley. Discipline and a lot of it. Clean your room. Attend all team meetings and be on time. Study. Make progress toward a degree. Prepare for exams. Take the academic side of college seriously. Attend class and be there every day. And finally, understand this, there are severe penalties in this program if you do not follow the rules. And the consequences of your failure to follow the rules are not pleasant. You will not like them.

It seemed as though with each passing semester I was running fewer and fewer stadium steps. In fact, I was hardly, if ever, in trouble any more. I actually got along with Port. When I would hear freshmen bad mouthing Port, I would just look at them and say, "What do you know about anything. You are just a dumb ass freshman with your head up your ass."

I could see what Port was trying to do…save them…just as he had saved me from myself. Port's great underlying message in all he did was this…Successful people are different from other people who are not successful in that they have learned to make themselves do the things success requires, while others simply have not yet developed the ability to force themselves to do those required things. The entire issue is about self-discipline.

At OU, both Bud Wilkinson and Port Robertson knew what the real magic elixir of a winning athletic program was…a program based upon teaching the players to be disciplined. Bud used to tell us this, "Men, we need to be in such great physical condition so we can take it to our opponents with a minimum 100% effort on every play. We will wear down our opponents mentally and physically so that when the fourth quarter comes, they will have doubts about whether victory is worth the physical price they must pay for it. And because we are the team with the most discipline, we will win."

Port was as vital a cog in the Wilkinson football dynasty as the line coaches, the backfield coaches, or anyone else connected with the program.

I am sure you are familiar with the much-used cliché, "the older I get, the smarter my parents become." This is especially true of Port and most all of the OU athletes who went through the PGR system. By the time I graduated, my hatred of Port had turned to respect, admiration, gratitude, and then came full circle to love. He was truly the man who saved me from myself.

Port Robertson did not smoke or drink alcohol. I am not certain but I don't think he ever missed a day of being on the job for the five years I was there. I never heard Port cuss either. Port was admired by Dr. George L. Cross, the President of OU, and by all of the academic community. They knew Port was even more concerned about academic progress toward degrees than almost anyone else in college sports at any college in the USA. Port was, at least in my mind, an exceptional man, no matter which way you would want to measure him...morally, intellectually, or spiritually. Port would have been in a pretty small group of exceptional folks.

When I was close to graduating, I knew I had one final obligation to fulfill before I could leave OU. It was to go see Port and thank him for all he had done for me. I will never forget going into his office. His office, in earlier years, had been a huge source of stress for me. I was usually in big trouble when I sat across from the imposing figure we called PGR. But this time a real serenity filled me. I started to thank Port for not giving up on me. I stopped and said to Port, "I have a question which I have wondered about for several years now. I would like to ask you, Coach, why are you so different than other men. You do not smoke, drink, cuss, and have a certain standard of excellence others do not possess. Why?"

I will never forget Port's answer. He looked at me and began to explain, "Well Johnny, several years ago I attended a meeting. I was told along with several other men that many of us would likely not be alive in 24 hours. I left the meeting and looked up into the sky and had a little talk with my maker. I asked him to spare my life the next day and if he would, I would live my life in such a manner that he would never regret having let me live. It was D Day and I would land at Normandy. I survived, Johnny." Port then looked at me and said, "And Mr. Tatum, the way I figure it, a deal is a deal."

The rest of the story is Port was severely wounded when a mortar round went off near his forward observation post. Port was on the field telephone barking off target coordinates when the round destroyed his radio and inflicted a life threatening wound to his right ear and earlobe. Port was in the hospital recovering for more than six months. He received the Purple Heart and several combat decorations for heroism.

Port never spoke much about himself. His focus was on the thing he loved most in life...the young and undisciplined athletes in all sports at OU. And Port was right...he did live his life in such a manner the Lord would have been proud of. Port is surely in heaven now, working with the new freshman classes coming in through the pearly gates...telling 'em the way it is in heaven.... God's way or the highway.

Before he died, I told Port how much I loved him and admired him. I told him how well prepared he had made me for the complex decisions I would make as the CEO of a large company. I carried Port with me my entire business career. The principles Port taught me were invaluable. I outworked everyone. I only spoke the truth so all I had to remember was what happened. And I focused on the things no one else would do and I did them. And perhaps Port's greatest lesson of all, I learned to give others all I could to help them learn to control their most difficult adversary...themselves.

When I go back to OU I keep looking for the most important statue of all, the statue of Port G. Robertson. There are or will be five statues of Heisman trophy winners. Those guys are immortalized because they are somehow the best college football player of the year. Maybe they were good enough to help their team win 11 or more games one year. And that qualifies them for a statue. Now I am not picking on Billy Sims, Billy Vessels, Steve Owens, Jason White, or Sam Bradford. I am just talking about a man so many of us truly love and appreciate...Port G. Robertson. A man thousands of us owe a great deal to. Some of us owe him for having giving us our very lives. Thanks, Port.

Hopefully then, someday someone will decide it is time for perhaps the greatest servant of OU athletics to have his own fitting statue on campus, perhaps near the library! That would be a place Port would feel at home. A place dedicated to learning and teaching. I know a Latin phrase appropriate to end this chapter on a man so many athletes loved and admired. It goes like this, "Bis vivit qui bene vivit." Translation, "He lives twice who lives well."

Port's life was a model for those seeking more than just the status quo to emulate. Port was a role model, a teacher, a coach, and a mentor to football players, wrestlers, tennis players, swimmers, golfers, runners, and baseball players. He made our lives more meaningful because he was a part of it. All that knew him, miss him.

Epilog on Port G. Robertson: One Christmas when I was living in Lincoln, Nebraska, probably around 1990, my phone rang. It was actually Christmas day. I answer the telephone, "Merry Christmas." The voice on the other end said, "Well, Merry Christmas to you, Johnny Edward Tatum." There are only two people in the world who call me by my full name, my mother and Port Robertson. I was stunned. Quickly I asked, "Am I in some kind of trouble, Coach?" Heck, I was 50 years old and terrified at the sound of Port's voice.

"No, Johnny, I just wanted to call and wish you a Merry Christmas." A warm feeling engulfed me. Having Port call with seasons greeting was a highlight of my life. It is still a precious memory. I have always believed maybe I was one of Port's greatest challenges. Perhaps I was sort of the model of "if I can succeed with Johnny Tatum, then anyone has a chance to make it."

I know at times when I was a freshman, I was a real load for Port. Thank God Port did not quit on me. Thank God he did not give up. I simply cannot imagine how my life would have been had Port not brought me to heel and to see the light. I know one fact, it would have been way less rewarding than it was.

I saw this saying once in a bank. I modified it some and hung it in my office and often said it to my kids. "Life is tough. But if you are stupid or stubborn, it gets a whole lot tougher." That saying sort of sums up the lessons of Port G. Robertson. His message could be summed up thusly... Just get it right the first time.

What a person Port was. No doubt about it, he was Bud Wilkinson's secret weapon. Port was Coach Wilkinson's Head Drill Sergeant, and Port was the most unique Drill Sergeant—ever! There are none like him and it is doubtful there ever will be another either.

Celebrating Port Robertson—an OU get together at the OU-OSU duel match in Norman

Port Robertson receiving Merit Award from OU Athletic Council, Jim Terry

BUD WILKINSON—THE GREAT WHITE FATHER

ALMOST TO A MAN, THOSE WHO WORE THE CRIMSON AND CREAM AND DID battle on the grass of Owen Stadium would say of our leader, the Great White Father, Bud Wilkinson was a man of few words. I asked his son, Jay, about his father being a man of a very few words. His response to me was, "My brother and I would say our Dad was very selective in his choice of words."

Jerry Pettibone was from Dallas Jesuit High School and was recruited as a running back to OU in 1958. Jerry played for four years and became a graduate assistant in 1962. His description of Coach Wilkinson was, "Bud was a 'Here is the plan type of man. This is the offense we will be running and any special plays and the defenses we will be using. Each assistant coach knows his area of responsibility, now go prepare your players to execute a winning performance.' He was not a micromanager."

Jerry went on to add, "Coach expected us to do our jobs, but if a player or coach was not performing at a high level of expectation, then Coach Wilkinson would not hesitate to intervene."

Using a military comparison, Wilkinson's style would have been a combination of a General Eisenhower and an Omar Bradley. In other words, a CEO like Ike and a get down in the foxhole with the soldiers like Bradley.

As a three year letterman, an offensive center, and a graduate assistant coach under the Great White Father, I only saw him really pissed off once. That was at Nebraska in 1961 when the Cornhuskers were leading the Sooners 14-0 at halftime. I can tell you this about that experience—you did not want to be around a completely pissed off Great White Father…ever!

A typical week of Bud Wilkinson Old School football would start on Sunday evening around 7 pm. Coach would be the entire program. He would lay out the offense, defense, and any special things about the team we were going to play. A complete scouting report was given to each player, highlighting the important aspects of the game ahead. One thing was for certain, Coach Wilkinson was a very well organized and thorough person.

During the season, his practice schedule was the same each week. Monday. The third team would scrimmage the Blue Boozers if the thirds had not played a significant amount in the previous Saturday's game. (The Blue Boozers were all the players who did not travel with the team or, at home games, did not play in the game. They would go out to Louis Bar and drink beer on Friday and Saturday nights. This group always wore blue practice jerseys.) On Mondays, the two alternate starting units would have a walk through practice of the offense and defense for the upcoming opponent on Saturday. Practice for the starting units…T-shirts and shorts. Practice would be about one hour in duration except for the thirds and Blue Boozers.

Tuesdays were the tough day, full gear dress. If there was any contact, it would be on Tuesdays. Practice time was a good two and one half hours. There was always a live run through of offensive and defensive schemes and lots of drills to keep fundamentally sharp on blocking and tackling.

Wednesday was an abbreviated version of Tuesday. Thursday was a review of the battle plans for the game on Saturday. Practice on Wednesday and Thursdays was about an hour and a half each day. Friday was a loosen up and pregame practice day, a run through again of the game play… duration, maybe 45 minutes. If we had already arrived at the away game location, Friday practice was on the home team's field.

Friday nights were always the same routine. After dinner on Fridays, we as a team would go to a movie. After the movie, we walked back to the hotel. There we would each receive two things—an apple and a pregame scouting report. Even for home games in Norman, the football team always stayed in downtown Oklahoma City at the Skirvin Tower hotel.

Coach Wilkinson had a police escort follow a special Greyhound bus to take us to and from Norman and the OU campus to Oklahoma City.

The meticulous attention to detail was a Wilkinson characteristic. Everything about him said that here was a very well organized person...his dress, his poise, his vocabulary, and his style. We had one or two coaches try to emulate him, but to no avail. There was only one Bud Wilkinson and nothing described him better than these four words...The Great White Father. For when he chose to speak, it was as if the clouds parted, and there was the word, and the word was from God. And we listened and when we were in his presence we were in awe.

As I write this, it was over 50 years ago that I wore the Crimson and Cream with a number 50 on the jersey and helmet. Remembering someone so long ago might be a tough job. Not so when it is a person so memorable as Bud Wilkinson. I have a couple of pictures of him and his coaching staff. Daily I will look at his picture and ponder the great life that I have been blessed with, and wonder just what my life would have been had the Great White Father not have played such a prominent role in it. Surely, it would have been different.

Bud Wilkinson—The Great White Father

SOONER FOOTBALL

Bud Wilkinson with Lavelle Sanford (JET's mother)

OKLAHOMA COACHES 1962 – L TO R, BUD WILKINSON, JAY O'NEAL, BOB WARD, GEORGE DICKSON, CHET FRANKLIN, RUDY FELDMAN, GOMER JONES AND EDDIE CROWDER.

A POTPOURRI OF OU THOUGHTS AND STORIES

THIS BOOK IS A POTPOURRI OF THOUGHTS AND STORIES. IT IS THE TYPE OF book a reader could pick up and begin to read on any page and it would make perfect sense. You could read it for five minutes and learn something or you could not put it down and read it straight through. Most of it is humorous and yet some of it is informative too. In this chapter, I will just throw some things together...most are completely unrelated.

THE MYTH OF WAHOO MCDANIEL

One of the biggest myths of OU football history surrounded former Sooner Wahoo McDaniel. The myth is that he supposedly ran from Norman to Chickasha once. The truth was...Wahoo ran part of the way. I talked to his roommate Bobby Boyd and Bobby said he gave him a ride for most of the way. It really did not matter. Wahoo was popular with the fans whether he ran all the way or not. Wahoo went on to pro football from OU and played for the Denver Broncos. He became a pro wrestler, too. He wrestled under the name, Big Chief Wahoo. I was scrolling through the TV channels one evening a long time ago and all of a sudden, filling my screen was none other than Big Chief Wahoo. I watched him pin his opponent with his famous Bow and Arrow hold. Wow. Just like the run to Chickasha...lots of fiction.

JOE WASHINGTON'S DECISION TO ATTEND OU

After I had retired and moved to Norman and lived there for about ten years, I volunteered and did some work for the OU athletic department. I made a new friend in former OU great running back Joe Washington.

I have met a lot of people in my life from all walks of life and I am here to tell you Joe Washington is a special person. He redefines warm and friendly. Joe is just about as nice as anyone I have ever met.

If you were ever fortunate enough to have watched Joe play football, what can be said about his skill that hasn't already been said? I was talking with some former teammates during an OU game when Joe was the star running back for the Sooners. Joe had just made one of his spectacular runs for a TD. One of my teammates, Leon Cross, asked me how I would have gone about tackling Joe had I played linebacker and tried to defend against him. I thought for a moment and responded, "I believe the only way I could tackle Joe would have been had I been armed with a sub-machine gun with at least six full clips of ammo." I had never seen anyone run like Little Joe could run, before or since. I cannot believe Joe did not win the Heisman Trophy. And the most amazing fact of all about Joe, he is every bit as nice a person as he was a great football player.

I asked Joe how he ended up playing for OU. He told me since he grew up in the Houston area of Texas, he just always sort of assumed he would play for the Texas Longhorns. When he was a senior in high school, he took his last college visit to OU. OU sent a private jet down to Joe's hometown to pick him up. When he arrived at OU he was picked up at Wertheimer field in Norman by one of Joe's college hero's, OU star running back, Greg Pruitt.

Greg pointed out to Joe that Oklahoma was such a fabulous place to live they had on the car tags, Oklahoma is OK. And, they wanted Joe Washington so badly they had named the athletic dorm after him—Washington House! Joe spent the weekend with Greg Pruitt and was truly impressed. Head football coach Barry Switzer said to Joe, "Can you imagine being in the same backfield with Greg Pruitt?"

Joe went back home on Sunday. On Monday morning, his phone rang. It was Greg Pruitt. The first thing he said to Joe, "Well, have you announced you are coming to OU yet?"

That made up Joe's mind and the rest is history. OU got a superb running back, but most important of all, they got one of the real gentlemen of all time to be a part of the great Sooner tradition.

Bobby Boyd #25—OU Quarterback in 1960 and later an All-Pro Corner Back for Baltimore Colts

Joe Washington and Barry Switzer

Greg Pruitt

Joe Washington turns the corner on another big gainer

OU IS LUCKY TO HAVE BOB STOOPS

As I write this book, OU head football coach Bob Stoops has won eight and lost eight bowl games. Some people say he is no longer Big Game Bob (but they can't overlook the magnificent 45-31 win over Alabama in the Sugar Bowl, keeping Bama from repeating as National Champions in 2013). They say he can't win the big ones anymore. Sometimes the pundits ask me for my opinion on Bob. My answer may surprise you.

I think Bob Stoops is one of the classiest OU head football coaches of all time. He is coaching in what is the most competitive and difficult time in the history of college football. The mere fact he keeps OU continuously in the top tier of college football programs is in itself at least a minor miracle. OU football is an annual sell out—standing room only!

And every year in the Big XII conference, Bob has had the Sooners in the hunt playing for the title.

As Bob enters his seventeenth season at OU in 2015, his record is 168 wins, 44 losses for a .792 win percentage. Bob reached 100 wins faster than any coach in college football history. He has won one National Championship, eight Big XII titles (twice as many as any other school in the conference), and had 75 NFL draft picks (13 first rounders). Not bad for someone playing in the talent laden Big XII conference with teams like Texas, Texas Tech. Texas A&M, West Virginia, Baylor, and Oklahoma State.

Yes sir, I believe OU is lucky to have Bob Stoops. He is a man of high principles. If one of his players violates one of the big NCAA rules, he will be shown the highway by Bob Stoops, and it does not matter how good a player he may be. He will not sacrifice the reputation of OU athletics for a cheap ticket to win a few games. Bob Stoops is better grounded than to sacrifice the future for the short-term gain. His teams play hardnosed football and are well coached. He generally plays a tough schedule, too.

Every year he has a couple of tough non-conference opponents. At a school like OU, he could schedule the Sisters of the Poor but he doesn't. I have met Bob Stoops and he has always been cordial to me. He is quick to recognize the contribution of past Sooner football players to the building of the great Sooner tradition. As a former OU football player, that means a lot to me.

Bob has offered the former players admission to closed practices any time they are in Norman and have the time to come out and watch the Sooners practice. That, too, is a nice touch by the Sooner coaching staff led by Bob Stoops. Bob Stoops is always quick to acknowledge all Sooner players from whatever era for their part in contributing to the Sooner tradition.

When I went to OU so many years ago and became a member of the Sooner football program, I had no idea just how significant it would become. Through the years, the fact I had played for OU under Coach

Bud Wilkinson opened many doors for me. The mere fact I had been associated with such a storied football program as OU said things about me that I did not have to say. In a very emphatic manner, my association with Sooner football sort of separated me from others, and in a good way. In those moments I was humbled by the significance of it all…its history…its tradition…and the Sooner magic.

As I said above, Bob Stoops is the current leader of the OU Football program. There are many qualities that this writer loves about Bob Stoops. Number one among these reasons would be how quickly Bob gives credit to all the past OU players for starting and building the OU tradition. And tradition is a very big deal in Sooner land. There are so many pluses for the Bob Stoops era one does not really know where to begin. Certainly Merv Johnson would be one place to talk about in the Stoops team.

Merv is the Director of Football Operations and is the color man on all Sooner football games. Merv hails from Mizzou where he played and coached. Merv proudly talks about getting to play against the undefeated Oklahoma Sooners and National Champions in the mid 50s. That would have been Jerry Tubbs and crew. And speaking of Tubbs, here is a story Jay O'Neal tells about Tubbs.

After Tubbs senior season, he was selected on the All American team and would play in the annual All American game against the Detroit Lions professional football team. On that same team of college All Americans was Paul Hornung, the All American QB from Notre Dame. The college all stars were practicing and it was time to practice punting. Tubbs was the deep snapper since he was the center. He could not center the football anywhere near the punter who was 15 yards back from the line of scrimmage.

A frustrated Hornung said, "Hey, what gives Tubbs, you are supposed to be an All American center."

To which Tubbs replied, "Well, at OU, the three years I centered we never had to punt." Makes sense to any well informed Sooner. When you go 47 straight wins, there really isn't very much of a need for a punting team or a kickoff return team, now is there?

But that was about another time in OU football lore.

IN BOB DEVANEY'S HUSKERLAND...

I have lived in Arizona, North Dakota, Nebraska, Iowa, Florida, and Alabama since I left OU in 1964. Everywhere I have lived, the people there wanted to know more about what it was like to have played for OU. One time one of our sales reps in Central City, Nebraska, Dick Evers called me and asked me to play in a Beef Club event that raised money to pay for the Nebraska University dining program for all athletes.

In the golf tournament one of the holes, a par five, was designated the "long drive hole." Being somewhat of a big hitter, I hit a very long drive on that hole and ended up winning the prize. Now significant was the fact that the legendary NU coach and athletic director Bob Devaney was the emcee of the dinner following the golf outing. It is also a material fact of this story that you know that Bob Devaney knew me well and knew that I had played against his NU teams back in the day.

When dinner was over, Bob took over and started the recognition phase of the golf tourney. Now the Coach had consumed one or two sarsaparillas and was feeling no pain. He came to the long drive contest and started to announce the winner. As he read the summary of the hole, he came to the name of the winner, stopped and yelled, "Holy Crap, the winner is John Tatum. Stand up John." So, I stood up and Bob said, "How many of you know this SOB?"

There was a sort of uneasy rumble through the room and Bob continued, "Hey, he played football for the enemy—Oklahoma!" The crowd of some 300 began to boo and throw napkins at me. Bob, however, was not through with me. "Come on up here John," the former coach said.

Then Bob put his hand on my shoulder and said, "Now, John, everyone knows how Oklahoma's players use steroids to improve their performance so, before you get this long drive award, you must piss in a jar, take the urine sample to a lab, and have it tested for steroids, or you can donate the prize that you have probably illegally won back to the Beef Club!"

I replied, "Heck of an idea, Bob...and Boomer Sooner everyone!" I was booed by the entire crowd, but it was sweet revenge and all in fun.

The legendary Bob Devaney, former Nebraska Head Football Coach and Athletic Director with JET

A "GREAT" RUNNING BACK

A "great" running back...the setting, Playboy Club in New Orleans. Old JET was attending a several week seminar at LSU on marketing insurance. A quick sidelight, I met another former Sooner football player who was also attending the seminar put on by the Insurance Institute and LSU. That player would become the OU Athletic Director several years later...Wade Walker. Part of the seminar was the attendees elected class officers. Wade was elected President and Old JET was elected Vice President.

But, back to the story and the setting...the Playboy Club. Since the seminar was several weeks in duration, several of us decided to drive down to nearby New Orleans. One of the class members just happened to be a Playboy key club member. He suggested we go to the Playboy Club and enjoy a really funny comedian playing there. So, we did.

The comedian, part of the way through his act, began to talk about a celebrity in the audience. As I recall, it went something like this, "Ladies and Gentlemen, we have with us this evening a great running back from the Oklahoma Sooners." All of a sudden, the comedian had my undivided attention. He continued, "Yes, ladies and gentlemen, this Oklahoma star back played in the early sixties for Bud Wilkinson's Sooners."

I thought, "Holy cow, this must be one of my teammates, or at least someone I know really well." I looked around the room for a familiar face.

The comedian went on and on about what a great running back was in our midst from OU! I could hardly wait to see one of my old buddies there in the Playboy Club. "So, without further ado, ladies and gentlemen, please help me give the former OU running back star and owner of New Orleans Tuxedo Wear, Richie Boudreaux a big hand."

And there he was, all decked out in black tie attire in all his splendor, with an entourage of about a dozen groupies, the one and only, Richie Boudreaux. Now just for the record, Richie was on the OU football squad. He walked on after serving a four-year hitch in the USMC. He wore jersey number 25 but never played even one down in any game during the 1962 season. We called him the old man of the team. If you were to press me to give you one outstanding quality of Richie, it would be he was a great guy and lots of fun...very very likeable.

Richie was out on the town when he appeared at the Playboy Club. Knowing Richie, the consummate promoter, he had probably slipped the comedian a fifty to promote Richie's business, the New Orleans Tuxedo Shop.

After the comic had finished his gig, I quickly made my way out to the lobby to wait for Richie and his group to exit. A short while and there Richie stood, face to face with his former teammate, none other than the Heavener Flash, Johnny Tatum. When Richie turned to face me to merely say that he was startled would be the understatement of the year. Richie was at a complete loss for words.

I interceded, "Richie, aren't you going to introduce me to your friends?" After a short burst of stammering and stuttering, Richie finally found the words, "Hey, everyone, meet one of my OU teammates, Johnny Tatum, one of the meanest linebackers I ever saw."

Richie Boudreaux's friends just couldn't get over the fact that two OU stars were here at the Playboy Club on the very same night. Before Richie and his group made their way to the exit, Old JET sent them on their way with this gem, "I really do not have the words within me to adequately tell you just what an exceptional running back Richie really was." And with that Richie whispered in my ear, "Johnny, I really owe you one."

Richie was not the only pretend OU Sooner I have come across in my travels. I have met several make believe or pretend to be OU Sooners. When someone claims to have played for OU, I quickly start a little game of "ten questions" and usually by the time I get to question two or three, the great pretender said something like, "Well, then I got hurt and had to quit."

If I ever did get to question number ten, it would be this, "Well, show me your knees." If there are no scars…he is most likely another great pretender. I should carry around a little CD player with the Platters song, *Oh Yes, I am the Great Pretender*.

Every year many of us gather for the annual Spring game and Varsity O Club Golf Tournament. Old warriors get together and tell tall tales about when we were young and daring and wore the Crimson and Cream onto the playing field. We relive the days of our youth and sometimes we were pretty good football players. We laugh and play together, bonded by the scars and great memories of Sooner football. We never really say it out loud but I know we love each other. We lived together and played together. We learned together and we sometimes suffered together.

We share a great many of the same memories. Memories of times when we were the architects of Sooner legends. We won some and we lost some. We were both Champions and also rans, but we were there and a part of the great Sooner Nation.

We were both spectators and participants. We made friends with other athletes…track guys, wrestlers, basketball players, swimmers, golfers, and baseball players. They were all Sooners and trying to make their mark. We are all enshrined at the Sooner walk of fame. Each of us, year-by-year and sport-by-sport at the southeast corner of Owen Stadium. It is a place you can go and find your year and stand looking at your name and remember when you were young and wearing the Crimson and Cream.

I once asked my grandfather, John T. Owen, Sr., what he thought success was. He told me that if you asked a hundred men, you would get a hundred different answers. Here was his answer, "I believe if right before you die, you can hold up one hand and name a close friend you have had in your life for each finger, then you have had a most successful life." I wondered about his definition for years. But the older I got, the more I believe his statement about success to be right on.

Now I am retired and the moments with good friends and family are even more precious. I once asked my great friend, Clyde Turbeville, what he liked most about retirement. He said, "You don't have to be around anyone you don't like." I like spending time with the most special friends in my life and making new special friends, too. I am tempted to list dear friends here but I won't for fear I would have a senior moment and forget someone like Bill Castles. And that would truly be tragic.

When I was still working, I would look forward to annual events when I would get to see my special friends, friends like old teammates, or work place peers, or fishing buddies. Now that I am retired, I can hardly wait for those annual events to roll around again. For three days each spring my teammates from the 1961 Sooner football team get back together to play golf and talk football and watch the latest version of OU hit the field. And most of us are there—Jimmy Carpenter, Bob Page, Leon Cross, Ron Payne, Tom Cox, Karl Milstead, Paul Benien, and John Tatum. And it just does not get any better than that. It seems only yesterday when we were students and athletes at OU. The tempus has really fugited!

And soon a new version of Sooner sports will be etching their contribution to the Sooner tradition in the history books. They will be creating their memories and as surely as anything, the time will pass too fast and someday they, too, will treasure the days when they were young and daring and wearing the Crimson and Cream. But for now, all that is important is the realization some young boy or girl is watching and dreaming someday they too can wear the Crimson and Cream. For it is true every boy and girl yearn for the day when they can wear the Crimson and Cream. Boomer Sooner.

Here is the epilogue to this chapter. Since Nancy Jean and ole JET returned to Mecca...aka Norman, each spring around mid-April, we host Karl and Barbara MIlstead from Wichita Falls, Texas. And we host Tom and Sharon Cox from Wichita, Kansas. And finally, we host Ron and Becky Payne from Breckenridge, Texas. All these men were teammates at OU. Karl still works and is a partner in Dry Forks Production Company in Wichita Falls. Tom is a retired bank president and Ron is retired from the Canadian Football League and was the past owner of a motel in Breckenridge, Texas. They are all guests over the 3-day weekend that features the spring game, otherwise called the Red/White Weekend.

REST IN PEACE

Bud Wilkinson	Gary Wylie
Gomer Jones	Don Dickey
Eddie Crowder	John Benien
Bob Ward	Mike McClellan
Jimmy Harris	Mike Ringer
Jerry Tubbs	Claude Hamon
Larry Grigg	Dennis Ward
Bill Pricer	Jim Grisham
Ken Northcutt	Larry Vermillion
Jackie Sandefer	Bob Kalsu
G.A. Lewis	Joe Don Looney
Ed "Wahoo" McDaniel	Phil Lohmann
Prentice Gautt	Port G. Robertson
Joe Rector	Ron Hartline
Duane Cook	Richie Boudreaux

Former Sooners that old JET knew who are now deceased.

WAS IT WORTH IT?

At the writing of this book, Old JET the author is 74 years of age. Here are some of my reflections as I look back to the days when I was thought to be indestructible. I started playing football when I was in the ninth grade and 14 years old. Football for the four years at Heavener High School was a real hoot. I was never hurt…it was fun for every moment I played. Then came college football at OU and under The Great White Father, Bud Wilkinson.

From the moment I stepped on the campus at OU, football became a serious business. Freshman football back in the day was like an intense version of a Marine Corp boot camp, only longer in duration. When I arrived on campus, late August of 1959, we were immediately issued full gear and practice started the next day. There were about 45 scholarship players on the freshman squad plus a number of walk-on players. We were not eligible to play for the varsity back then.

Practices were five days a week and about two hours per session. Port Robertson was the freshman coach and had a crew of graduate assistants helping him. No one ever said this, but football season lasted until the Varsity was done with their season. We played two games, one against Tulsa University and the other against the rivals at Oklahoma A&M (Stillwater).

Port mainly put us through endless drills…blocking, tackling, and conditioning. His ulterior motive may have been to run off those who could not or would not get with the program. There were many casualties.

From day one, the athletes at OU were regimented. It was like being at a military school. Our rooms had to be clean, beds made, clothes hung up in the closet, and no clutter. We had to take a grade sheet around and have our professors put down our grade, how many times we had been absent, and any pertinent comments. And there were disciplinary consequences for those who did not measure up to the program's standards… stadium steps! I've already discussed those so won't repeat it here.

The harsh regimentation culled the squad quickly. Four years later, my freshman class had 11 who had survived the OU football program.

The 64,000 dollar question…was it worth it. I am only going to list the injuries I suffered in my three varsity years of playing football for the Oklahoma Sooners. I did not suffer any injuries as a freshman. As a varsity player, I had four knee operations, one separated shoulder, a broken nose, separated sternum, broken left foot, several broken fingers, lost four and a half teeth, and suffered at least three major concussions.

It is difficult to say whether or not I would play again if I could do it all over again. The camaraderie in and by itself would be hard to trade. Good lifelong friendships are invaluable. And several of my teammates have become lifelong friends…no, make that great lifelong friends. So far the only lingering side-effect which has effected or limited my activity is arthritis in my back. The condition no doubt came from the beating I took in football. I can no longer play golf and that is a real bummer.

I cannot say that playing football at OU was a real asset in my career. My career took me out of Oklahoma to Arizona, North Dakota, Nebraska, and Iowa. In those states, OU football was no more than an "Oh, an OU football player, big deal!" The only place different was Nebraska, but there I tried to keep my playing at OU a secret as OU had a heated rivalry with the Cornhuskers.

The companies I worked for tended to be more attuned to agricultural schools. I realize that many ex-athletes are quick to credit "their college days as an athlete" for their success in business or their career, whatever it may have been. This was clearly not the case in my career. In my case, an agricultural background would have been the major advantage for me to have possessed. I had little experience in the Ag related fields.

So, "What's it all about Alfie," is pretty much, at least in my case, just football itself. Unlike high school and junior high, college football turned out to be quite different. It was a full time job and that job had many hazards. It was, to say bluntly, dangerous and very risky for a relatively small player like I was back then. As an athlete at OU, I felt as though I really had two full time jobs, one as a student and the other as an athlete. About all I did along with my teammates was, eat, sleep, practice, and study...24 X 7. For me in particular, throw in rehabilitate for, after all, I was a consensus Johnson and Johnson All American...this was for those college athletes that used the most tape and protective gear in order to be able to play the game of football.

Back to the main question, was it worth it...the beating, the injuries, the after affects? Second guessing is not really my thing. My old and dear friend Charley Elliott told me this one time as we discussed a "what that might have been."

Charley said, "I would rather be sorry for the things that I have done than to be sorry for the things that I wished that I had done but did not do." Not bad advice. I once heard a noted scholar discussing the topic of taking chances. He cited a study done on a thousand senior citizens, all age 75 or older. The question they were asked, "What is your chief regret in the life you have lived to date?" The number one answer is very thought provoking. Number one was, "I would take more chances!"

My great uncle Al Robertson, when once advising me reminded me of this jewel, "You can't steal second base with your foot on first." And so, would I do it again...subject my body to the torture of being a Sooner? In a New York minute I would. A New York minute by the way is the elapsed time between when the traffic light turns from red to green and the car behind you honks!

When one considers all the sum total of the athletic experience at OU, being a football player under Bud and Gomer and getting to know Port was a million dollar deal for me. And if it taught me anything at all worthwhile, it was discipline. And in the big game of life, great self-discipline will carry you far. Port taught us that doing the little things matter. Things like keeping your room clean and learning is more important and education is perhaps a number one priority. Bud and Gomer taught us that whether you think you can or you cannot, you are probably right. So, success is a mind over matter deal. And most important of all, we athletes were surrounded by some of the very best influential people that ever came down the pike! Bud Wilkinson, Gomer Jones, Port Robertson, Jay O'Neal, Bob Ward, Ken Rawlinson, and JD Roberts.

So, listen up all you Sooner Slobberknockers. When the Pride of Oklahoma forms the interlocking OU and strikes up *Boomer Sooner* as they march off the pregame field, I stand up along with 86,000 other Sooners, a lump comes up in my throat, and a tear in my eye, and I feel very blessed that I am at home in my Sooner Nation!

WHERE ARE THEY NOW?

Dr. Rick McCurdy, Surgeon, Norman Regional Hospital, Norman, Oklahoma. Tight End. Resides in Norman. Could actually read and write. Chose Med School over the NFL.

Lt. Col. Bill Hill, US Army Ret., Retired Banker, Ada, Oklahoma. Played both ways at O Line and Defensive Tackle. Lives in Ada. Famous for having played with little or no eyesight…a braille tackle if you will. Known for crippling some of his own teammates by mistaking them as the opponents.

Charley Mayhue, Attorney at Law, Ada, Oklahoma. Halfback & defensive back. Still active In Mayhue Law Practice. Lives in Ada. Mostly looks after Bill Hill.

Glen Condren, aka, "Moose." Retired among other things from the NFL where he played defensive end. Glen lives in Metropolitan Tulsa. Has recurring nightmares about Bob Ward slobbering on him.

J.D. Roberts, Active in the Drilling Fluids Business. Former Head Coach of the New Orleans Saints NFL team but best known and appreciated for getting JET out of Heavener and on a football scholarship to OU in 1959! Considered as JET's guardian angel. Lives in Oklahoma City. Won Outland trophy in 1953.

John Porterfield, aka the Phantom. Retired Assistant Superintendent, Owasso Public Schools, and Owasso, Oklahoma. Lives in rural Oolagah, Oklahoma where he raises horses. Played tight end and

Defensive end. Most famous though for rooming with the Heavener Flash!

Karl Milstead, aka Popsey Whopsey or Homestead. Partner in Dry Forks Production Company in Wichita Falls, Texas. Plays lots of golf and is widely known to be the greatest 14 handicap golfer to ever play the game. Played guard and place kicker, once kicked successfully a 7 yard field goal.

Big Ron Payne, aka Mister Catfish. According to legend, the greatest hands to ever play tight end in the Wilkinson era, at least according to his lovely wife Becky that is. Mister Catfish starred as a defensive end in the Canadian Football league for almost a decade. After a successful football career owned and managed the Ridge Motel in downtown Breckenridge, Texas. Known as a great Philanthropist, Payne supplied his Alumni Golf teammates with gifts like golf towels and hats from the Ridge motel. Wow, what a guy.

Billy White, aka Whitey Boy. Captain of the '61 Sooners. A product of the infamous Joe Kerbel of Amarillo High School. Loves snake jokes. Ring leader of the Texas four gang...Milstead, Cox, Payne, and White.

James Hardy Payne, aka Jimmy or Your Honor...US District Judge in Muskogee. Became semi famous for putting away desperadoes from Heavener. Philanthropist who conspired with a fellow donor to fix the Heavener flash up with a warm coat as a freshman at OU.

James Parker, aka Country....a Sweetwater Texas product. And like Jimmy Payne, a freshman Philanthropist who supplied the coat for the Heavener Flash. Resides back home in Sweetwater, Texas and is retired from the Raytheon Co.

Bill Watts, better known as Cowboy Bill Watts of the professional wrestling world. Played tackle at OU during the Wilkinson era but was too dangerous to be turned loose in games, he was known to bulldog opponents and render them helpless with his famous "lasso hold." Retired now, Cowboy Bill resides on the Emerald Coast in the Florida Panhandle.

Thomas Cox, aka Thom...Another product of Joe Kerbel and Amarillo High...Roommate of Whitey Boy. Thom made headlines as an OU tackle due to a serious injury. Headlines read, "Sooners to Play K State with Cox Out!" Thom is a retired Bank President living in rural Wichita, Kansas.

Jerry Pettibone, aka Jerry. Played Halfback and was the players' nominee to Captain the Blue Boozers. Pettibone a team favorite, scored a meaningless touchdown against powerful Oklahoma A&M with four downs from the two yard line and received high fives from his admiring teammates. Jerry lives in Norman.

Jay O'Neal, Jay and his sidekick, Jerry Pettibone, head up Sooners Helping Sooners, an enterprise to help ex-Sooner athletes find jobs after leaving college or professional sports. Sooners Helping Sooners is a 501C3 tax-deductible organizations. You can reach Sooners Helping Sooners by calling 405 236 1636.

Leon Cross, aka Rugged. After playing for almost a decade, the Old Rugged Cross was elected Captain Emiratis in his 7th or 8th season as a guard for the Sooners. Many teammates thought Cross was a player/coach since he was almost on social security. After an extended playing career he leveraged his longevity to full time coaching and later as an Athletic Director. Cross, now retired and devoted to promoting men's Gymnastics here in Norman, is arguably the Oklahoma Sooners number one fan in all sports.

Geary Taylor, aka Bear...thought by most teammates that he had either no oars or at best only one oar in the water! His bride has complete support of all who know her husband that she should be admitted to Sainthood! Taylor clearly is the classic person who broke the mold when he was made. When in his presence, all wonder what he will do or say next, he is the most unpredictable person in the world. He resides in South Texas and is a successful businessman.

Owen Hewitt, aka Bully. Bully was a track and field manager in the late 50s. Since always picking on others, he was assigned the nickname of Bully. Bully is a retired IT guru and lives in Norman with his dog Freckles.

Paul Benien, aka Doc. Paul must have been a right end as was Rick McCurdy, as the really smart players were right ends. Both Paul and Rick had great hands like Mister Catfish, but the right ends could also read and write. Dr. Benien still practices medicine in Oklahoma City.

William Wayne Lee, aka Jock Lee...All American Center at OU, one of the two smartest players on the team. The other, naturally, was the alternate center, the Heavener Flash himself. Football coaches always put the smartest players at center as they must be able to count up to three in the snap count. Some think the QB's have to be able to count, not so cadence breath, they just go once the center has decided it is time to hike the ball. Wayne is retired and lives in Boulder, Colorado where he was an architect designing hospitals and health care facilities.

Jimmy Carpenter, aka .Carp. Two sport star at OU...Halfback in football and center fielder in baseball. Oil Barron residing in Edmond, OK.

Marshall York, aka .Mr. York. Big strong tackle who was like

John Wayne toilet paper, doesn't take any crap off of anyone! Another

Amarillo High product of Joe Kerbel. Captain of the 1960 Sooner football team. Became a Tire Magnate in the Texas Panhandle. Retired and living the dream in Amarillo.

John Edward Tatum, aka The Heavener Flash. Known by teammates to be "swave and deboner", and possessing a way with words. A friend to all and indebted to JD Roberts for getting him out of Heavener. Retired and living in Mecca…the home of big time OU football, basketball, baseball, track, gymnastics, wrestling, women's basketball, and a personal favorite…rowing.

John Porterfield #82 and Glen Condren #88

L-R Jerry Pettibone, Karl Milstead, Tom Cox, Ron Payne, Johnny Tatum

OLD SCHOOL VS NEW SCHOOL

EVEN THOUGH THIS BOOK IS PREDOMINATELY ABOUT OLD SCHOOL OU football, here are some thoughts about some of the current OU football players. How are they different and what makes them better players than the old school OU players of a half-century ago?

In a word, there is little or no comparison. Arguably, even a great running back like Billy Vessels probably could not make a Bob Stoops scout team. Now that statement will likely infuriate the Old School readers. But it is probably true.

Let us compare a current running back to a 1950s running back. How about Samaje Perine—5'10" x 235 or 240 pounds, can bench press 225 pounds ten times and three sets. Old School players did not even have weight training.

Let's go back a couple of decades and compare Old School with Sooner running back Joe Washington. Little Joe was a pure runner who beat many a defender with raw speed and elusive running. One tackler trying to down Washington had but two chances to actually tackle Joe in the open…slim and none! What Joe or Samaje did to opposing defenses was against modern one-way defensive killers. Contrast that to Old School players who went both ways.

Another case in point, the Old School OU players who actually went to the NFL were mostly defensive players…even well-known OU backs, when drafted by NFL teams, opted to play defense in the pros. Two well-known examples are Clendon Thomas, an Old School legend OU running back, third on the OU all time backs and average yards per carry list, and Bobby Boyd. Boyd, a quarterback from Garland, Texas, became an All Pro corner for the Baltimore Colts.

In comparison to Old School backs, old JET will concede that some

Old School backs were almost as good, even close in some cases, to the modern Switzer-Stoops running backs. When we move to the big uglies, that story changes big time.

Old School linemen on both sides of the ball were, for the most part, not even close. The size, speed, and strength of the Switzer-Stoops era are night and day different. A typical offensive line of Stoops vintage will look like this…average height 6'5" and average weight would be about 325 pounds, and it is not unusual to have tackles that are 6'7" by 350 pounds! A typical Old School O Line might average about 210 pounds per man.

The defensive side of the ball would be even more lopsided in favor of the Switzer-Stoops era players. Just consider the difference in the game today vs the Old School days. Today, the game is played using every single square inch of the field, end zone to end zone and sideline to sideline. Defensive backs must have speed and quickness galore and be open field whizzes in tackling ability. Linebackers today are larger than old school D Tackles and have the speed of Old School backs and ends.

It is fun to look back on from whence we came in a game we love to talk about and compare to other times. Someday, these Switzer-Stoops Sooner stars will be Old School as the game gives way to new innovative thinking and rules changes to make the game even more different than ever before. The stadiums will keep getting larger so more fans can enjoy Sooner football.

And writers like old JET will try to explain just what happened and how Sooner Magic won another victory for the good guys. The truth is, who cares who was the best, as generation after generation of Sooners keep adding their contributions to the great Sooner tradition.

Another way to compare Old School with Stoops era Sooner Football is just plop in a DVD and watch some Old School football being played 50 years ago…BORING! With the change in rules that allowed unlimited substitution, we saw the metamorphosis of a completely different style of football. And, one very significant thing happened. College football began to compete with NFL football for TV audience. As offenses continued to change and open up, the fans got a new type of football to watch. Wide open attacks featuring great running backs, sure handed receivers, and gun slinging quarterbacks. Games likely to end up 50 to 49 with fans on the edge of their seats wondering if their favorite team could just hold on and win!

TV started to control what games were televised and at what time of the day. The college football product was so good; college football was on TV starting Thursday, and Friday, and Saturday, and the cost of going to see your favorite teams began to skyrocket. It took big bucks to keep the coaching talent in place, let alone the new facilities.

Football had really come of age when the former defensive back from Iowa came to town. Bob Stoops was full of Sooner Magic. He and his coaches began to recruit NFL style players. Premier running backs like Adrian Pederson and Demarco Murray…Quarterbacks like Sam Bradford and Landry Jones…and O Lineman and D Lineman who are now marque players in the NFL. One recent NFL draft saw the 1st, 3rd, and 5th draft choices all Sooners.

Owen Field on Saturdays looked like a pro football event—86,000 OU fans there to see their Sooners do their magic. Sold out games were the norm. Sooner football had become a great product. Everyone, especially Sooners, love a winner. Bob Stoops' Sooners destroyed Alabama in the unforgettable Sugar Bowl. The Sooners were more than just impressive; they were seemingly unbeatable.

There is a line in the movie *Patton* that is appropriate for the Sooner diehards. Patton tells a story about the victorious warrior returning from battle with prisoners in chains, chariots with gold and silver and other captured treasure in them—the commander riding in a chariot with two white horses pulling it. A captured enemy is standing in the chariot next to the commander holding a laurel wreath over his head and whispers in the commander's ear, "All glory is fleeting!"

Bob Stoops and his Sooners would come back down following an 8 and 5 season. Hopefully the team has learned an important lesson. That is, there is plenty of room at the top, but you will find no seats to sit down there. Perhaps when spring ball starts, Coach Stoops should resurrect the Bird Story or the Ben Hogan story. The Old School was better at one thing than either Barry or Bob—WINNING…like three National Championships and 47 straight.

All I know is back in a time that seems not so long ago, my teammates and I played and sometimes we won and sometimes we lost. But we always tried as hard as we could to win. And in the end, our teams won two Big 8 championships out of four chances. We were part of the Sooner story. Now we are getting older and we are saddened when another Sooner warrior is no longer with us. But that is life and just as the seasons change, another Sooner football team will hit the field and, in their way, will be showing 86,000 raving fans a new way to use Sooner Magic to add new chapters to Sooner football.

The bottom line is, we just want our players to feel the Sooner enthusiasm and electricity in the air when the referee blows his whistle and drops his hand and it is kickoff time in Owen Stadium once again. The Pride of Oklahoma strikes up with Boomer Sooner, the crowd goes wild, and our favorite time of the year is finally here once again.

OUTNUMBERED IN NEBRASKA

LIVING IN NEBRASKA WAS GREAT EXCEPT FOR ABOUT FOUR MONTHS during the fall and early winter. I am talking about football season and Huskermania! For everyone and their dog in Nebraska are football fans. And those NU fans were sort of like some religious groups that peddle their brand of religion door to door. From the moment I arrived in Lincoln, Nebraska, the Big Red Nation began their attempt to recruit me and make me a rabid NU fan like they were.

For example, let's talk about the 1987 showdown with arch-rival Oklahoma. Oklahoma had defeated their in-state rival, Oklahoma State (A&M) the week before the big game with Nebraska by a 29-10 score. The win against OSU wasn't without severe cost. The Sooners lost their starting Quarterback, Jamelle Holieway, and key fullback, Lydell Carr, to injuries.

Nebraska previously had been ranked nationally #2 behind OU who was #1. NU was vaulted ahead of OU prior to the November 21st showdown. It was billed as the Game of the Century Part II.

The odds makers made the Huskers a 7-point favorite. The polls, because of the loss of two OU key offensive players, their ace wishbone QB and their punisher blocking and running fullback, had dropped the Sooners to #2 and elevated NU to #1.

The Husker faithful could not keep their mouths shut. The week before the Game of the Century Part II was filled with optimism that this year would be different. Their defensive standout and loudmouth end, Thomas, boasted, "OU will not win in our House!"

Someone who worked for the Company that I was the CEO of in Nebraska had changed the light switch in my office. It proclaimed, "Nebraska turns me on! Oklahoma turns me off!"

A local TV station interviewed me before the game and wanted to know how it felt to be the only avowed Sooner in Huskerland. But alas, a true Sooner cannot be converted to any other football team…ever.

And so it was with JET, Crimson and Cream forever. When someone would tell me how OU was going to endure its all-time butt kicking, I would simply warn them of the impending "Big Hurt!"

The game finally arrived and the Game of the Century turned out to be exactly what Old JET had warned so many of the Husker faithful… watch out, you are just setting yourself up for the Big Hurt. And so it was!

Barry Switzer brought his fired up Sooners to the land of the Corn Cobs and with substitute QB Charles Thompson and backup fullback Rotnei Anderson at fullback spelled just another mixture of Sooner Magic. And old JET was there.

When it was over, the Stadium in Lincoln, Nebraska sounded like a cemetery…all you could hear was the shuffling of feet. And every few moments you could hear one of the emotionally spent Huskers yell out, "Those lucky bastards!"

In a post-game interview, OU defensive end commented, "The Nebraska players should have spent the week prior to the OU-NU game practicing rather than talking." And that would have been even truer about their fans. OU Defensive Coordinator Gary Gibbs had designed a perfect defensive scheme to thwart the NU offense which held the Huskers to only 7 points.

The Lincoln Journal Sunday edition ran an ad for a souvenir offer to remember the big win over arch-rival OU. Talk about jumping the gun. However, it was typical of Husker-mania.

And for one more year I would listen to music in my ears, a chorus of Huskers singing, "Just you wait until next year."

The following day…the Sunday after the Big Hurt, was a very busy day. I did two things that day. I baked a giant cake, made it look like a football field with icing. Across the cake's football field I wrote, OU 17-NU 7 and under that I wrote…THE BIG HURT! I put the cake near the entrance of the office for all my forlorn beaten down Husker friends to see. And in addition, I had signs throughout the office with quotes from the people that I worked with stating just exactly how NU was going to destroy my beloved Sooners. Come Monday morning, I would have my cake and eat it, too. Being outnumbered in Nebraska was a wonderful thing and I loved it.

It was during basketball season when one day my phone rang. I was still living in Nebraska. It was my old OU teammate and great friend, Leon Cross. Leon was an associate athletic director at OU and was calling to ask if I would like to go to the OU—NU basketball game at the Devaney Center in Lincoln on Saturday night. I accepted and the two of us sat right behind the OU bench. When a timeout was called, OU coach Billy Tubbs would stand facing the fans and his team, which were seated facing their coach. As Billy talked with the team, some NU fan started throwing ice at Billy. When about the third chunk of ice hit him, Billy stopped talking and went down to the end of the OU bench and got Kevin, the Oklahoma State Trooper (Highway Patrolman) by the arm and the two marched back to in front of his seated players. Billy pointed to the crowd and said to Kevin, "Some son of a bitch is throwing ice at me, Kevin. I want you to stand here and catch the son of a bitch and when you do, take out your pistol and shoot the bastard!"

I told Leon, "If Kevin shoots someone, I think you are about to have a public relations nightmare!"

The truth is, Nebraska fans are the same type fans as the OU fans are—both sets love their team. It is sad that NU departed from the BIG XII. When that came down, it destroyed an American institution—the Thanksgiving Day football game between rivals NU and OU.

I no longer live in Cornhusker land and, to tell the truth, I really miss my Big Red friends—Tom Banderas, John Best, Ryan Rohl, Doug Gibson, and Denise and a whole bunch more. And to all of them, Go Big Red.

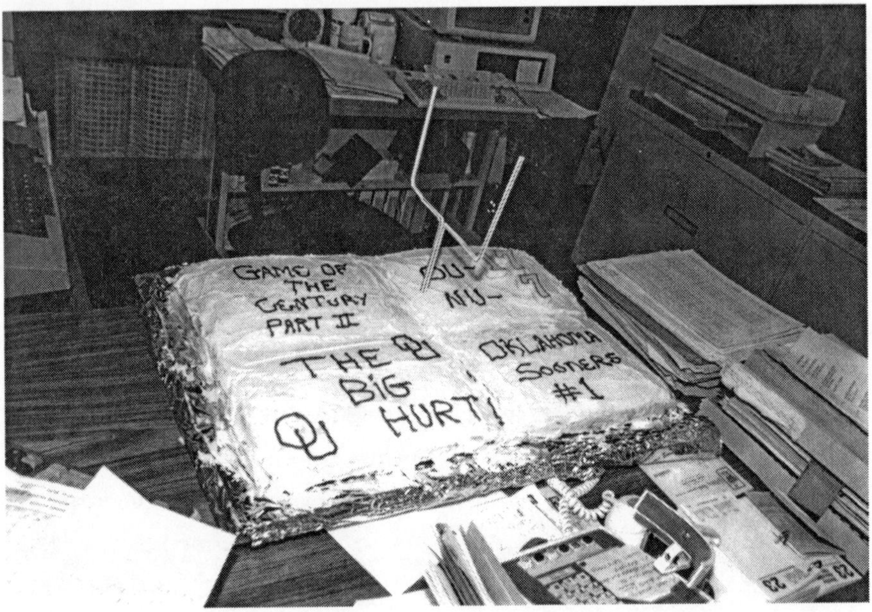
GAME OF THE CENTURY PART II
THE BIG HURT!
OKLAHOMA SOONERS #1

ALL JETCETERA TEAM

Down through the years, people have asked me about the great players I either played with or against. I will start with the greats we played against. Arguably we played on the field of battle against some really great players. Here is the JETcetera list of great opponents.

From Kansas, Gayle Sayers, John Hadl, and Curtis McClinton. From Pitt, Mike Ditka. From Alabama, Leroy Jordan and Joe Namath. From Mizzou, Johnny Roland. From Nebraska, Bob Brown. From Syracuse, John Mackey and Jim Nance. From Notre Dame, Nick Bonaconti.

And from the OU varsity/alumni game, former OU greats…Tommy McDonald, Jim Weatherall, Kurt Burris, Clendon Thomas, Billy Pricer, Jimmy Harris, Ed Gray, Billy Krisher, and some I cannot recall.

I played with some really great players as well. Prentice Gautt, Bobby Boyd, Ralph Neeley, Ed McQuarters, Lance Rentzel, Ronnie Payne, Carl McAdams, and Jim Riley are just a few OU stars that went on to the next level…NFL or CFL.

Here, though, is my special All JETcetera Football team. There are players from Bud, Barry, and Bob's eras.

OFFENSE FIRST…

Ends: Eddie Hinton and Keith Jackson
O line: Bill Krisher, Ed Gray, JD Roberts, Jammal Brown, Ralph Neeley
Running backs: Tommy McDonald, Joe Washington, Steve Owens, and Prentice Gautt
Quarterbacks: Jimmy Harris & Sam Bradford
Kicker: Uwe von Schamann

DEFENSE

Ends: Steve Zable and John Flynn
Tackles: Leroy Selman and Jim Weatherall
Nose Tackle: Tommie Harris
Linebackers: Rod Shoat, Jerry Tubbs, and Bob Harrison
Corners: Bobby Boyd and Ricky Dixon
Safety: Roy Williams and Clendon Thomas
Punter: Joe Don Looney

Any all-star type team becomes immediately debatable. This one is no exception. However, this would be a very formidable team to play. Old JET played against some of these guys and can testify that most are certifiable card carrying killers on a football field. Most notable among the group, Jimmy Harris never lost a college football game while playing for the Sooners in the mid-fifties. Harris was the field general who directed most of the 47 straight victories at OU, a record still standing in Division One Football.

And here is a thought on Sooner recruiting areas. A question first... what is one of the most rewarding areas of any state to recruit quality football player talent? I will bet you, the reader, are thinking some place in Texas or perhaps southern California. Wrong! Here is my suggestion for a cannot go wrong recruiting area, the old Oklahoma Black Diamond Conference area—Sallisaw, Poteau, Heavener, Stigler, Hartshorne, Spiro, Muldrow, Stilwell, and Eufaula.

Here are some players from over the years from these towns. Just their names say enough...going way back...from Poteau, Bob Loughridge (Tackle), David Rolle (Fullback). Next, from Sallisaw, Steve Davis (Quarterback). From Heavener, John Titsworth, (Defensive Tackle) and Johnny Tatum (Center/Linebacker). From Spiro, Rod Shoate (Linebacker). From Muldrow, Glen Condren (End). From Stilwell, John Garrett (Center). And last but certainly not least, from Eufaula, Lucious Selmon(Nose Tackle), Dewey Selmon (Defensive Tackle), and Leroy Selmon (Defensive Tackle), and J.C. Watts (Quarterback and former Congressman)! Some diehard Sooner fans believe that Leroy Selmon may have been the greatest Sooner lineman ever. At any rate, not a bad group of players from the foothills of the Ozarks and small town America.

Ralph Neeley, All-American at OU and All-Pro with the Dallas Cowboys

Keith Jackson, All American at OU and NFC Rookie of the Year

THE FRIENDSHIP OF FRANK AND HENRY

I DON'T KNOW WHEN OR EVEN HOW THE CAMARADERIE BEGAN AT OU. Maybe it was a spin-off that just happens to teams as the players interact with each other. Many of my teammates at OU feel as I do that the bonds of we Sooners set us apart from other football programs.

While writing this book, I heard a story from a former OU football player. In order to protect his identity, we will just call the two individuals Frank and Henry. Both Frank and Henry are former OU footballers. Frank worked his way up and became a three-year letterman, contributing much to the OU program. Henry was not that fortunate as he was injured and then reinjured. Finally the coaching staff released him from the squad, but Henry retained his scholarship and finished his degree at OU.

Both players, after graduating, went their separate ways and became very successful in their respective careers. Frank stayed active in OU events like the Varsity O and other University clubs. Henry, on the other hand, did not feel comfortable with being involved, especially with athletic alumni groups since he did not really ever participate as a varsity athlete. But Henry was a huge success story and played no second fiddle to any OU alumnus when it came to post-graduate achievement.

As this story deepens, after Henry and Frank had retired and looked for worthwhile ways to spend their time, they each was drawn back to the one thing that brought them to know one another so very long ago... OU athletics. The OU Red/White spring game draws former athletes from all sports back together for all sorts of events. On Friday before the game on Saturday, there is a golf tournament that is a big scramble with former teammates playing together.

As luck would have it, Frank and Henry were paired on the same team and actually rode together in the same golf cart. It was like old home week between the two as they shared with each other where life's journey had taken them. An old friendship was rekindled. The mutual respect was definitely Old School!

It has now been more than ten years since Frank and Henry ran into one another at the spring Red/White event. The once casual friendship is a rip-roaring example of the deep friendships that exist between OU athletes. Camaraderie—hardly, more like love and deep respect for one another.

Frank and Henry now face a different adversary, father time. More and more teammates are facing new foes like Alzheimer's and other challenges. They are just a part of getting older. As Henry ages and battles his own aging issues, he did call time out and thank his old buddy Frank for making him feel so appreciated and welcome home to OU so many years ago on the golf course. Frank's take on reconnecting with Henry is, "My life has been enriched because of my old and dear friend Henry!"

No doubt about it, Bud Wilkinson, Gomer Jones, and Port Robertson taught us more than to block and tackle. In their strange way, they taught us to value and respect one another.

When you analyze it all, football, Old School is about the team. And as someone most eloquently said, "There is no I in team." In football there are eleven players from one team in the game at one time. The Great White Father was fond of saying, "Come on men, everyone must go full speed, if one man loafs, he lets the other ten men down…everyone must do their part in order for the team to succeed."

Being able to depend upon ten other players is perhaps the building block of camaraderie. When we consider the aspects of real teamwork manifested, how about this example of Old School Football…47 Straight Wins! Camaraderie begins with a commitment between teammates. And perhaps it is a strong bond…unbreakable in Old School teammates. How else can anyone attempt to explain 47 straight wins…a winning streak that has stood among NCAA Division 1 schools since 1957!

If for no other reason, football at OU, for me, was the genesis of many enduring friendships. In conversations with many OU fans and other just football fans, I often cite the number of very close friends that I have with OU ties. And I am not referring to casual type friends. We are talking special family type closeness. I believe it is friendship on the same level as combat veterans have for one another. Some of these friendships go back to an OU beginning some 56 years ago. I do not have enough fingers and toes to count them all.

When we are together, no matter how many of us in the group, there is a warm feeling, a special one, that makes you know it is a very special time, for that is how being in the presence of great friends makes you feel. It is a red-letter day in every way…and the sort of day you don't want to ever end or forget.

Maybe being a part of a team and tradition like OU football molds you into that type of thinking…thinking that instills the notion that teamwork is more important than anything else.

The special friendships were the final stage of the metamorphosis we all went through as we became Sooners so many years ago. And if we are lucky, we will all meet again and again, and laugh together, reliving so many good times so long ago, and missing our teammates who are no longer with us.

SECTION TWO
HIGH SCHOOL FOOTBALL
THE BEGINNING OF THE COLLEGE FOOTBALL DREAM

HIGH SCHOOL FOOTBALL
THE BEGINNING OF THE COLLEGE FOOTBALL DREAM

IF YOU LOVE COLLEGE FOOTBALL, YOU KNOW THAT THEIR TRAINING grounds and farm system come from the local high schools all over America. Virtually all young men looking to play football at any level of college or in the pros got his start on his local high school football team. It could be a historically powerhouse high school program like some in Texas, Oklahoma, and California, a small unheard of program like I came from in Heavener, or any school in between the extremes.

Few high school players make the major college ranks, even fewer make it into the NFL or CFL. Despite the odds, untold thousands of young players dream of wearing the colors of their favorite college team.

More than likely, the head coach, if not most of the coaches, on high school football fields all across the country teaching the new crop of football players played football at some level in college. Thus, football is a closed loop system—high school players go to college and some get their teaching degrees and return to high school to coach the next generation. Football is a lifelong passion—some are fortunate enough to not only play it, but also get to coach it.

Johnny Tatum fits that mold. After a year as a graduate assistant at OU, he entered the high school coaching ranks. This section will be focused on his success there.

But first, read on for some thoughts that will be helpful to today's high school football players who aspire to play Division I college football.

RECRUITING FORMULA FOR PLAYING DIVISION I FOOTBALL

THIS CHAPTER IS FOR ASPIRING YOUNG FOOTBALL PLAYERS WHO WANT TO play big time college football. These special players dream of someday running through the tunnel onto the natural grass of Owen Field in Norman, Oklahoma and being a member of the Sooner Football team. In this chapter the requirements are laid out and reveal what it takes, position by position, in order to dress in the Crimson and Cream of the Sooners.

Meet Jerry Pettibone, legendary recruiter for big time programs— Oklahoma, SMU, Texas A&M, Nebraska, Northern Illinois, and Oregon State. At Texas A&M, Coach Pettibone was named by Sports Illustrated the top recruiter in college football. The number of All Americans Jerry Pettibone recruited is too long to list here. So, any discussion of recruiting led by Coach Pettibone carries with it instant credibility. If you are a grandfather seeking to help a grandson or a dad wanting to see your son play at a high level, then this chapter is a must read for you.

John Tatum and Jerry Pettibone were teammates at Oklahoma University in the late 50s and early 60s. Jerry learned his offensive and defensive tactics from two of the football gurus of the time, Bud Wilkinson and Gomer Jones. Jerry went on to work under some of the great coaches of the time. In addition to Wilkinson and Jones, add Haydon Fry, Barry Switzer, Jackie Sherrill, Jim McKenzie, Chuck Fairbanks, and Tom Osborne. If a person wanted someone to paint a picture and describe what a tight end or a running back or a tackle or center would look like, you could not find a better artist than Pettibone.

But first, let's review some football rules and limitations on recruiting that all Division One University schools must obey. The NCAA impossed a limit of 85 scholarships on its member schools. This is a big deal. Consider…11 offensive players plus 11 backups for offense, that is 22 scholarships. 11 defensive players plus 11 backups, that is 22 more. We are at 44 scholarships. We need special teams for kicking extra points and field goals with some back ups, say 15 players, now we are at 59 players. We need a kickoff receiving team and a kick off cover team, say another 11 to 15 players. Now we are at 70-75 players.

A college typically recruits incoming freshmen, of which of a class of 20-25 new players, most teams will be lucky if 6-10 players possess the needed skills to compete as freshmen. There are a couple of exceptions to throw into this discussion, the hardship case and the medical scholarship.

First, the hardship case. If a player is injured in the first 20% of the season and with a doctor's statement it is proven the player cannot return to play the remainder of the season, the player is awarded another year of eligibility. Different from this is the player who sustains a career ending injury. This player is awarded a medical scholarship and it is not then counted as part of the 85 scholarship limit.

So, each year a college team may only be able to recruit a few players in a given position. There is little room for error in big time college recruiting. When you factor in injuries, the recruiting game becomes even more critical.

Having said that, let us examine the fine details of criteria to play at a high level and the position requirements necessary to be a good bet to play at least two or more years successfully. The selection of the best athletes, position by position, is the prize. Picking the best amongst the very best is the winners reward.

Every position has a set of requirements. Specifically size, speed, build, strength, athletic ability, attitude, character, academic standing, and family to name some of the criteria the college recruiter looks for in prospective athletes. Because the talent factor is critical in a team's ability to win games, coaches and programs must rely upon their ability to recruit and develop their scholarship players. Some coaches bad mouth and belittle the star rating systems used by recruiting magazines to rate players by position and number of stars. Recent studies show a high level of correlation between the four and five star athletes and the players ability to become a Sunday afternoon player (NFL).

Before we get to specific measurement of different criteria, there is one very important caveat. Often a college will recruit a player with a low rating and develop him into an excellent player. The rating service perhaps had the player rated a two or three star player. A college with excellent top notch position coaches have a knack for developing players. Players from small high schools or players who did not play but a few years of football are often great candidates to develop into outstanding players.

Late bloomers are also candidates to outperform the rating the player had been thought to be. Just because a rating service had you ranked low doesn't mean that individual is destined to be an also ran. A great attitude along with a great work ethic goes a long way toward becoming a great player. A young person needs to constantly hear this saying…the harder I work, the luckier I get.

At OU in the early 80s there was a running back from the Houston area named Greg Pruitt. Greg was too short as a running back but former OU star QB and assistant Coach Jay O'Neal said, "Greg Pruitt is a great example of a player who doesn't measure up on a certain criteria but his athletic ability trumps everything else and smart recruiters see that difference manifested on the field." In the old days, O'Neal said, "Recruiters would ask high school coaches, who was the best player you played against this year?" If the recruiter for that area got a name, then off they went to recruit that player.

Today, the top Universities have "evaluation days" where they put aspiring college players thru drills which measure the important characteristics, position by position.

One last thought. When a high school player signs a letter of intent to attend a college and be a scholarship student athlete and they fail and quit the team, they were either recruited wrong or trained wrong. It is clearly a coaching mistake. Programs where the head football coach accepts this reality are the really good programs in the country. In this regard, this author credits Bob Stoops and his staff with top grades for recruiting quality. The proof is in the pudding—more Big XII titles than any other program.

If your son or grandson wants to become a highly sought after high school football player, they must score high on the criteria evaluation sheet. They must show a dominating level of proformance in their high school highlight discs.

Let's take a look, position by position, at the different criteria used by Pettibone and colleges to assess players and positions. First, let us start with the big uglies…the offensive lineman. The centers and left tackles are similar but the other interior lineman are about the same for each other. The left tackles must measure up in order to be a five star prospect. Here are the "must haves" for the left tackles. These are must haves because if your quarterback is right handed, on drop back passes, the back side of the pass rush must be blocked by the left tackle. Therefore, the most important skills left tackles must have are first, size—at least 6'4" but preferably taller. 6'7" would be better. Wing span is also important in being able to block the backside rush by the defensive end.

Right in there with size is foot speed. Great offensive tackles have great foot speed and different drills point out foot speed, from excellent to poor. Another way to say it, offensive linemen need to be light on their feet. They need to be good dancers! Being able to move your feet in all directions is a number one priority for left tackles. Being nimble is a must for left tackles.

Most generally, size with regard to weight would be in the 300 pound area. But if a tackle is 6'6" plus 285 with great wing span and super foot speed and agility, we are talking five-star player. For left tackles, everything hinges on the players ability to protect the blind side of the drop back quarterback.

The center, like the left tackle, must have good foot speed. Size is not as important as it is for the left tackle although it is somewhat important. The center must be athletic and show this athleticism in a variety of line drills. Being light on your feet is important for centers. The center must have good recogniton ability, for they usually set the blocking schemes for the O Line. Intelligence is at a premium for centers.

For aspiring centers and left tackles, consult with your local high school coaches regarding the line drills which are used to build and develop balance. Then go to work at improving your control over your feet. Being able to control your own agility through drills is a lineman's goal. Balance is the key asset. Being able to change directions at a high rate of speed says you possess outstanding control of your feet, and that you are worth a gamble to the college recruiter.

Here is a great tip for all players. This is a drill an aspiring athlete can do just about anytime and any where. It is jumping rope. This drill can work miracles at developing a condition called, "being light on your feet." Become an expert at jumping a rope. Set a goal to be able to jump non-stop for five minutes, then ten, then twenty, then thirty. Jump with just your right foot, then your left, then with both feet, then running. In no time at all, you will start to become light on your feet. Your balance will improve dramatically.

In evaluting backs and ends, the aspiring athlete must consider his skill set. What type of player does he see himself as. For example, does he have straight line speed or is he a run to daylight type player. Take, for example, former OU great players Greg Pruitt and Joe Washington. In 1972, the two backs were featured in the same OU backfield. Looking at both players you could quickly ascertain they were two entirely different type of runners. Pruitt was small and was primarily a north south runner. If Pruitt could get to the corner of the defense, no one was likely able to catch him with his 4.3 speed. Greg was small but deadly fast.

On the other hand was Little Joe Washington, the eventual runner up for the Heisman Trophy. Joe was a run to daylight type runner and arguably maybe the best ever. But if speed was the main criteria for running backs, Little Joe would have never run down the tunnel onto the sacred grass of Owen Memorial Stadium because with his 4.7 speed, well now sports fans, he was just too slow.

This illustrates the critical difference in types of running backs. For history would probably place Joe Washington in the top 20 of all running backs to ever play Division One football.

So, what's it all about, Alfie? In the recruiting arena, the high school athlete must determine what category or type player he is and then assess the D-1 schools that play offenses that feature backs and ends with the aspiring skill sets. After all, a player has to match up with a certain offensive type. And the more skill match ups which a high school player has with a college offense, the more attractive a potential scholarship offer might be.

In the Wilkinson era, Mike McClellan was a great example of straight line speed. Mike was the fastest running back that Wilkinson and the Sooners ever recruited. Mike was Olympic sprinter fast, winning the 100, 200, and anchoring the 400 spint relay team in Texas High School track. Offering a Mike McClellan a football scholarship was a cinch bet. Another running back out of Abiline, Texas was Jimmy Carpenter. Carp did not possess the straight line speed of a McClellan, but rather Jimmy was a run to daylight type back. He was as sought after a recruit as any back in the nation, proving the desire by Division One schools to go after backs possessing different skill sets.

No matter what position a high school player plays, if he is quick, has great balance, can catch the ball, has speed good enough for the position played, and is academically good enough to stay eligible, then chances are someone will offer him a scholarship.

Last in this section about recruiting is the most sought after of all scholarship players, the quarterback. The QB is, without a doubt, the most evaluated player of the lot. While size and arm strength are important, both of these physical aspects wane when compared to the number one trait a QB must possess.

We are talking about leadership. The search is on for all types of clues into a potential college QB's leadership ability. How is the player's grades. What type of extra curricular activities does he participate in? Do his fellow players look up to him and does he inspire confidence in his team mates? Once he satisfies the leadership component, what about his skill sets and do they match up with the offensive demands the college QB must be able to deliver?

You must see the connection between the skill sets a potential player has and the position demands of the college team. There has to be a match. So, it is always a what do you have in the way of skills and what does the college team interested need? One thing is for certain though, if you are a dedicated athlete who works hard at being one of the best, and God has blessed you with a high level of ability and your parents' gene pool endows you with a certain great body type, then some college will be looking at you to solve one of their position needs.

Everyone is looking for talented and motivated players who are good citizens. Staying out of trouble is a very big deal. No college wants to recruit an athlete who is trouble.

To end this chapter, I will take from its beginning and share with you my favorite Jerry Pettibone story. One late summer day my phone rang in my office in Lincoln, Nebraska. It was my longtime and dear friend, Jerry Pettibone. Jerry was the head football coach at Northern Illinois and had a favor to ask of me. Would I agree to talk with his team on Friday before the NIU Huskies played the Nebraska Cornhuskers on Saturday afternoon. I agreed to do it.

That Friday arrived and I went to the stadium in Lincoln as their practice was ending. Jerry introduced me to the team as his former teammate at OU and told the team that I played Nebraska in this very stadium and know what that experience is like.

I gave the Northern Illinois team my best ten minute Knute Rockne speech. The next day, game day, the game started and Northern Illinois was playing lights out football. At the end of the first half, the score was Nebraska 17, Northern Illinois 17!

The second half started and Tom Osborne must have cast a spell on the Huskers as they took no prisoners in the second half and ended up scoring several unanwered touchdowns to rout Northern Illinois.

On Monday morning I called Jerry and said to him, "Jerry, what in the world did you say to the team at half time? We were on the way to one of the great upsets in college football history so what in the world did you say to them at halftime?"

We both had a good laugh but the truth is, when two teams play and one has great desire and the other is talent rich, the talent rich team nearly always wins. The message is this, recruit talented players and they will generally make their coaches look a lot smarter than they really are.

Here is one final point and a plug for my OU teammate Jerry Pettibone. When Jerry retired from college coaching, he started a recruiting service. If you need help, contact "The Jerry Pettibone Group, LLC." Their telephone number is 877-220-2030. Jerry charges a fee for his service. He has helped many want to be college players secure scholarships to all levels of colleges. Jerry has a web site, just google up The Jerry Pettibone Group, LLC. The web site will answer most of the questions you might have about Jerry's service.

PERFECT PRACTICE—HEED THIS ADVICE

MY MOTHER WAS AN EXCELLENT PIANIST. SHE STARTED PLAYING THE PIAno at age five. Whenever she was at a function and there was a piano in the room, she became the entertainment. She was truly gifted in that she could read music or play by ear virtually any song she had ever heard. Inevitably someone would say as they listened to my mom play, "I would give anything if I could play like you!" When the person walked away, my Mother would turn to me and say, "If they had practiced as many hours as I have, they could play like me." If I heard her say that once, it was at least a thousand times.

I am not for sure I really understood what that sort of practice meant. I was probably too young. My understanding of the value of practice came to me when our neighbor's daughter, Sara Jane, and her new husband came for a visit to Heavener. His name was Bernard "Tut" Bartzen. Tut was the number one ranked clay courts tennis player in the USA. Tut gathered up a bunch of local boys, all about my age, in our early teens. We would gather at the local tennis court by the First Baptist Church and Tut would hit tennis balls to us. We would try to hit them back but usually we could not.

He would bring a stack of newspapers and put them down at strategic places on the service court. He would literally shred the papers with his serves. His practice sessions would last for hours. All of a sudden my mind connected with what practice really meant. It came to me like a ton of bricks hitting me. I got it. If I wanted to excel in anything, I needed to develop a passion for practicing. It was just that simple.

From that moment on, I became a fanatic at practice. I worked especially hard at drills designed to sharpen the skills needed for whatever sport I played at the time. As I aged, I noticed that professional athletes were masters of the basic fundamentals of their sport. Coach Wilkinson and all the OU football assistant coaches drove this saying constantly, "Practice doesn't make perfect, only perfect practice makes perfect!"

So, if you have a son or daughter or friend who thinks they want to become a much better athlete, instill within them the value of perfect practice. If you can get that done, you may be lucky enough to see them run down the tunnel or out on the floor as the band plays our State song…Boomer Sooner!

I was lucky in that I had the opportunity to be at the Masters Golf tournament on two different Saturdays. I spent a couple of hours watching different golf pros hit practice balls. They all practiced about the same. They would take out a five-iron and would hit about six or eight five-iron shots. When they finished, you could have put a small blanket over the eight balls. Every shot was the same. It was a perfect example of perfect practice.

Every sport has basics that must be mastered. And when they are, you become a very well-honed machine as an athlete.

THE DAY I BECAME A COACH

WHEN I GRADUATED FROM OU, I TOOK A JOB AS OFFENSIVE LINE COACH and defensive coach at Star Spencer High School in Oklahoma City. I was also the head baseball coach. At Star Spencer, I always had baseball players who could play the game. In 1967, we made it to the State Regionals and lost. I had most of that team returning in 1968.

Baseball season started at Star Spencer in March. We would go to southern Oklahoma and play some early March games. The '68 season began with high expectations. My entire infield was back, along with an ace right-handed pitcher named Rusty Hall. Rusty was a tall rangy kid with a great fastball and nasty offering of different breaking pitches. He could throw an overhanded curve ball that looked like it rolled off a table. Several big league teams were interested in Rusty. He was without a doubt one of the very best high school pitchers I ever saw.

But it wasn't just a team with good pitching. I had great players at key positions. My third baseman was Donny Grice. He would go on and play AAA baseball for the Oklahoma City 89ers. He would have made it to the big show but for his lack of speed. I used to say I could time Donny in a hundred yard dash using a sundial. He had a rifle for an arm, was good with a glove, and was a super switch hitter. Donny may have been my best baseball player ever. If he wasn't, then it was shortstop Mike Robinson. He had all the skills plus great speed. He was New York Yankees center fielder Bobby Mercer's first cousin.

We opened up the season and barely beat a poor team. We did not play well at all. This was my fourth year at Star Spencer and I knew my players well, except for the younger players on the team. Then a few days later, we lost to an even poorer team. The game was played on our field.

Afterwards, I kept the team on the field for some extra work. The fact was that I was pissed…really pissed that we had lost a game we should have won. After about an hour of infield and work, I called everyone in and was giving them hell when my shortstop, a junior named Mike Robinson raised his hand. I asked him what he wanted. He asked me if he could say something. I said sure. Mike dropped a big bad bomb on me.

He said, "Coach, you are telling us that we are the problem and you are probably going to kick me off the team, but I have to tell you that you are the problem. You yell and scream at these young guys and make them so nervous they can't play. When you yell at me it doesn't bother me or any of us older guys because we know that is just the way you are. But with the young guys, you should be encouraging them and not yelling at them. That is all I have to say."

That speech by Mike Robinson ended the practice. That was on a Friday and I stewed all weekend about what Mike had said to me in front of the team. I would ponder, "Who does he think he is anyway? I will kick his little ass off the team first thing Monday morning."

Then a little voice would whisper in my ear, "Yeah, but Mike is right."

I struggled all weekend with those words Mike had said about the baseball team and me. Deep down inside me, I knew Mike had been right about me. I was trying to coach like Bob Ward at OU. But these were 15-17 year old boys, not 21-year old men. There is a big difference emotionally between college men and high school boys. And it took a 17-year old named Mike Robinson to teach me what had been a hard lesson. My young player had to embarrass me in front of the team to get my attention and change my behavior.

Monday came and I called the team together at the beginning of baseball practice. This is what I told them. "First of all men, I want to tell you how brave Mike Robinson was for saying what he said. And I want to tell you Mike was right in what he said. Today I will make this team a promise, from this day forward, I will be your biggest supporter and encourager.

"From today forward I have but one objective and it is to help make this the most fun baseball season you have ever had. If you will try your best, I will try my best. If we both try our best, that will be good enough for me. Is that a deal?"

Each nodded yes. We were a new team beginning that day. My confession was magic. You could see the change in the team immediately. The kids were smiling and having a good time. They were loose and not up tight. It was a change in atmosphere and just what the doctor ordered.

We started to play the type of baseball the team was capable of playing. We started to not only win, but to dominate other teams! The Bobcats of '68 had started playing to the high level I expected of them, and were having fun playing. Rusty Hall, our great pitcher described above, was a junior and arguably the best right-handed pitcher in Oklahoma.

We managed to win the district championship and went to the regionals. We ended up playing Bishop McGuiness High School in the finals of the regionals. It was one of the best baseball games ever played in Oklahoma High School baseball. Neither team deserved to lose. It should have been the finals of the State AA Championship. The game went 16 innings. It was played at the Star Spencer field but McGuiness was the home team as they won the toss.

The hitting by both teams was scarce, and the fielding was superb. Both teams played more like pros than high school kids. It was a classic pitcher's duel. McGuinniss had a left-hander and Star Spencer had their ace on the mound, Rusty Hall, the 6'2" 185 pound ace.

The game was scoreless going into the bottom of the 13th inning. McGuiness had runners on first and third with one out. I called time out and went out to the mound. I called my infield in and reviewed what everyone did on a bunt. Everyone in the stadium knew Bishop McGuiness was going to squeeze bunt the runner home. If they scored, the game is over.

I went over the strategy. The first baseman, Freddie Emberson, was to charge the plate and cover the first base line. The second baseman, Robert Waller, was to break to first and then up past the mound to cover the left side of the pitcher. The third baseman, Donnie Grice, was to break towards the plate and cover the third base line. And my pitcher, Rusty

Hall, was to throw it high, hard, and tight, trying to force a pop up then break straight right toward the third base line. My catcher, Larry Gianfillippo, was to cover the plate. We were ready.

Rusty fired the first pitch high and tight, just like we wanted. The McGuiness hitter somehow got his bat up and squarely on the ball. It shot off his bat and split my third baseman and pitcher. My shortstop, Mike Robinson, was breaking on the pitch to third base. He saw what happened and changed his angle as he broke on the ball. Mike possessed all the attributes that really great infielders have…a great arm, a good glove hand, and outstanding speed and quickness.

Mike charged the super charged bunt and bare handed the ball on the dead full out run. He threw to the plate side armed and under his left arm. He hit Gianfillippo's mitt with a perfect throw. Larry had positioned himself right in front of the left front side of home plate. Gianfillippo was a carbon copy of Roy Campanella, short and squatty with lots of muscle and plenty of courage. He liked to punish runners when he tagged them.

The McGuiness runner slid into home and the plate umpire yelled, "You're Out!" Mike Robinson may have been the only baseball player in Oklahoma who could have made that great play that kept us in the game.

Rusty Hall struck out the next hitter and we were off to the 14th inning. In the top of the 16th we managed to score two runs and won the game 2-0. McGuiness' left-hander went the distance, as did our right-handed ace Rusty Hall. But it had been our shortstop and team leader, Mike Robinson, who once again saved our season. This time he did it with his speed, hand eye coordination and arm…not his courage. He kept us alive in the state tournament and the dream lived on with the Bobcats to win their first ever team State Championship at Star Spencer High School.

The state championship game was played against Choctaw High School, on their home field. Once again we were the visiting team and hit first. When I called the team in to announce the starting lineup and hitting order, I played a hunch I had. I said, "Leading off tonight is our center fielder, Steve Goff." Steve had hit in the seventh or eight slot all year, but Steve had been tearing the cover off the ball in the playoffs and I had a feeling he would save his very best hitting for his last game as a senior.

For some reason, the game was delayed in starting. Steve had his bat and was pacing around the batter's box. Finally he signaled to me that he wanted to talk to me. Coming in from the third base coaches' box, I met Steve half way between third and home. Steve said, "Coach Tatum, are you sure about me leading off?"

I looked at Steve and said, "You are the best hitter on this team right now. I know you are going to play your best game tonight. I can feel it, Steve, and I am just never wrong about these feelings. Now just get in that batters box and take three good cuts at the ball and enjoy this night. It will be a special night, one you will never forget, Steve. Savor the moment, Steve…this is a night you will always remember. It is special. Few people are ever in this type of place and time."

He hit the first pitch deep off the center field fence for a stand up triple. I can still see the big smile on his face as he came into third base. And the butt kicking was on. The Star Spencer Bobcats won their first state championship in any sport in the history of the school in the spring of 1968. My starters you know except for Terry Mason who played left field and Ronnie Simpson played right field along with others.

We did not lose many games that year after I became a real coach. It was not only a fun season but it was in every respect a great season. We beat teams with players like Darrell Porter and New York Yankees center fielder Bobby Mercer on them.

Coaching the Bobcat baseball team in '68 was a dream season. My infield was defensively superb. Freddie Emberson and Donny Grice were at the corners, both seniors. Mike Robinson at SS was a junior. Robert Waller at second base was a sophomore but was already a seasoned player. Nothing got past Robert. My outfield was anchored by senior Steve Goff. Steve had excellent range and a good arm. Terry Mason and Ronnie Simpson were both juniors. My catcher, Larry Gianfillippo was a sophomore but like Waller he had played a ton of summer baseball and played more like a senior than a rookie sophomore. Larry was built like Roy Campenella, short and squatty. He was quick and had a rifle for an arm. No one stole second base on Larry.

At the end of baseball season I was named the Oklahoma Coach of the Year. I always figured the trophy belonged as much to Mike Robinson as to me. Sometimes what you need to hear is not necessarily what you would like to hear. Sometimes it takes real courage for one to speak up and say what needs to be said. I was lucky I had such a player on our team.

I learned in the spring of '68 that the main objective of high school sports is to have a good time and enjoy those special years when you are young and dreaming big dreams. I learned the players at Star Spencer who played baseball knew how to win and, most important of all, they wanted to win. They just needed a coach who was smart enough to not get in the way. I always figured my team in '68 at Star Spencer was so good, anyone could have won the state championship with them. I do believe it became the most fun baseball season ever for the 1969 Bobcats.

STATE CHAMPIONS BASEBALL CLASS AA 1968

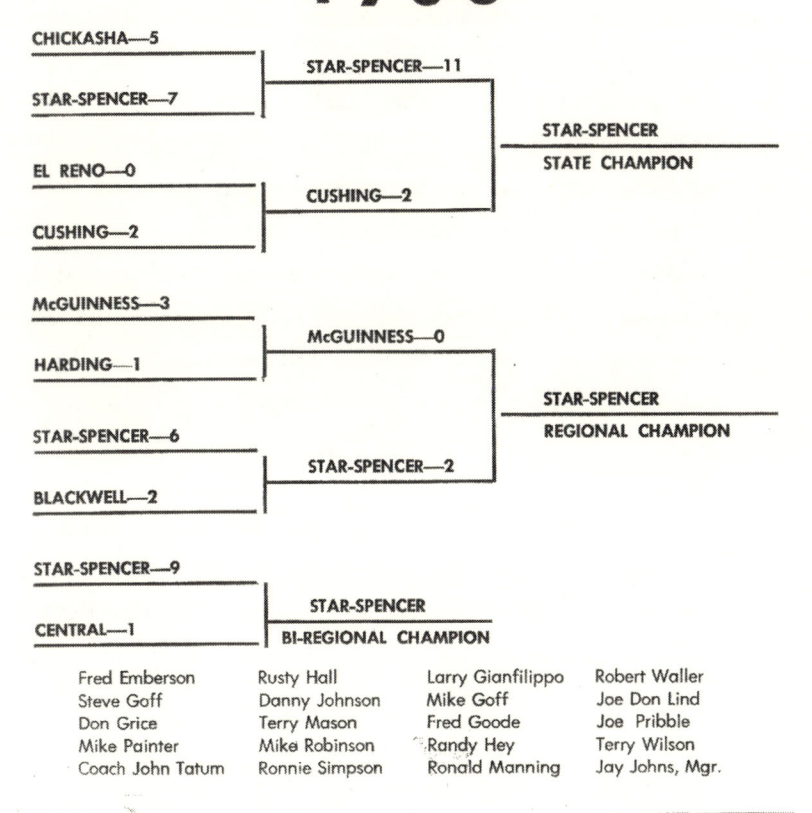

```
CHICKASHA—5 ─┐
             ├─ STAR-SPENCER—11 ─┐
STAR-SPENCER—7 ─┘                │
                                 ├─ STAR-SPENCER
EL RENO—0 ─┐                     │  STATE CHAMPION
           ├─ CUSHING—2 ─────────┘
CUSHING—2 ─┘

McGUINNESS—3 ─┐
              ├─ McGUINNESS—0 ─┐
HARDING—1 ─┘                   │
                               ├─ STAR-SPENCER
STAR-SPENCER—6 ─┐              │  REGIONAL CHAMPION
                ├─ STAR-SPENCER—2 ─┘
BLACKWELL—2 ─┘

STAR-SPENCER—9 ─┐
                ├─ STAR-SPENCER
CENTRAL—1 ─┘       BI-REGIONAL CHAMPION
```

Fred Emberson	Rusty Hall	Larry Gianfilippo	Robert Waller
Steve Goff	Danny Johnson	Mike Goff	Joe Don Lind
Don Grice	Terry Mason	Fred Goode	Joe Pribble
Mike Painter	Mike Robinson	Randy Hey	Terry Wilson
Coach John Tatum	Ronnie Simpson	Ronald Manning	Jay Johns, Mgr.

RAGS TO RICHES AT OKEMAH HIGH SCHOOL

I LEFT STAR SPENCER AFTER THE '68 SEASON TO BECOME HEAD FOOTBALL coach at Okemah. Okemah had not had a winner in almost 20 years. It would be a real challenge to build a program there. But I was heeding Gomer's advice. I was not following a winner. The coach I followed still ran the single wing. Modern football had not made it to Okemah until I got there in the summer of '68.

At Okemah I found kids who wanted to play good football but suffered from neglect. Immediately, I put in a weight program. I designed some weight machines and the VoAg teacher Ray Holman's FFA boys built them for me. The Okemah Sports Booster Club helped me pour concrete and set up the machines. Several of the boys I put on diets of peanut butter sandwiches at night before bedtime. Some of the kids were not getting enough protein in their diets. I got some commodity peanut butter for my poor Indian and white kids. Along with an intense weight training program, my football players began bulking up.

I was the head track coach, too. I instituted a rule that if you wanted to play football at Okemah, you had to run track. I wanted to accomplish several things my first year. I want bigger faster stronger players. My first year the offensive and defensive lines probably did not average 165 pounds. But we had fun playing football at Okemah and Mike Robinson would have been proud of me.

We taught a plethora of new drills which both offense and defense needed fundamentally. Our practice sessions looked like a mini OU practice...lots of drills stressing skill-building fundamentals.

By the end of 1968, our players were starting to play like seasoned athletes and our weight program was starting to build muscle. My players continued eating peanut butter sandwiches before bedtime for extra protein and they looked like football players the following year. My line averaged about 200 pounds and my backs were about 175. Every player who started on offense and defense could press 200 pounds or more. It was a magnificent transformation.

The season of 1969 looked to be promising. I had most of my team returning from the learning year before. A new multiple offense was something way different than any Okemah player had ever been a part of. The defense was made up of lots of stunts and different fronts—complicated and required a strong learning curve. One thing I picked up on quickly were the two unique team leaders I had. One was my quarterback, Ron Cottrell, and the other was a starting tackle named Robert Ambrose.

Cottrell was a junior and Ambrose a senior. Both would be the valedictorians of their graduating classes. I had the smartest two kids in the school on the starting line up. Robert learned all the offensive and defensive line assignments for every position and Ron learned all the backfield assignments for offense…. backs and ends. We made very few assignment type mistakes in '69.

We played our way into the District Championship title game against Tecumseh. Tecumseh had a running back in '69 named Harvey Ryan, the fastest high school runner in the USA. He had won the 100-yard dash that summer at the AAU meet in Eugene, Oregon. We were going to play them at our field for the conference championship. All week in practice I told the team, "Do not worry about Harvey. I have ordered rain for the game and the field will get all muddy and Harvey will run like an old plow horse."

With God as my witness, the referee blew his whistle and dropped his arm to signify the start of the game. Simultaneously there was a clap of thunder and it started raining as if on cue. It rained and rained and rained some more, close to three inches during the game. There were times you could not see across the field. Harvey Ryan got loose early in the game and went about 80 yards untouched, but there was a motion penalty and the play was called back.

We trailed late in the game. The field looked like a swamp. On fourth down, Tecumseh was going to punt out of the end zone. I called time out. I got my defense over on the sideline and told them, "Look, we are behind five points and need a touchdown to win. Do not block this punt out of the end zone. We will get two points and they will kick off from the twenty. The field is too muddy to sustain any type of drive. So, let's rush the punter and force him to run out of the end zone but whatever you do, do not tackle him in the end zone. If you do, we will lose. When he gets out of the end zone then cream him. If he looks like he is going to fall down in the end zone, catch him and don't let him go down. Everyone got it? Well, go get 'em."

We rushed the punter and unbelievably flushed him out of the end zone. When he crossed the goal line about five Panthers tackled him. It took three plays but we scored and won the game by a couple of points. To this day I do not know why the Tecumseh coach did not take a safety. Had he done that, they would have surely won the game.

It was a hard fought victory and district championship for my Okemah Panthers. It would be the second best season in the 63-year history of the school. My starting lineup was: Ron Cottrell-QB, Butch Standley-FB, John Martin-TB, Tommy Rickner-Slot back, David King-Wideout, Sam Palmer-TE, Robert Ambrose-T, Terry Goode-G, Jimmy Bishop-C, Duane Hibbs-G, Dal Campbell-T. Campbell and John Martin were tough kids, really tough and team leaders. Really good tough football players. Jimmy Bishop and Dennis Benson were outstanding young linebackers who improved almost daily.

When the seniors at Okemah were freshmen, Tecumseh beat them in a junior high football game by 60 points. Three years later, when these same guys were seniors at both schools, Okemah defeated them. What a turn around. In just two years, the Okemah players had become bigger, stronger, faster, and extremely well motivated.

We won the conference championship and went on to the state playoffs. In the first game of the playoffs, we lost on a really bad rule. At the end of regulation play, the game was tied. Back in '69 there was no sudden death playoff. The tie was broken statistically. The first criteria was penetrations, which was how many times did you cross the other teams twenty yard line. The penetrations were tied at four. It went to the next criteria, first downs, and those were tied too, at about 20 each. Then it went to the third criteria, yards rushing. We lost on yards rushing.

I always thought the criteria should have been total offense. We were a multiple offense and threw as much as we ran. Our offense was balanced and yet we lost on a criteria that measured only one aspect of offensive performance. But that was the way it was and our football season ended on a tie. Sort of like kissing your sister, not much of a thrill, more obligatory.

The Okemah Panthers served notice in '69 to all teams they played. There was a new era that had been born in '69. It was modern sock 'em in the mouth football. No longer would the Okemah Panthers be an automatic win for whoever played them. When you hit the field with the Panthers, you had better cinch down your headgear because someone was going to knock you into next week.

Winning the conference championship was a huge improvement over my first season at Okemah. My first year, the team went 3-6-1. Nubbin Duke and David Duke were about all we had. David Duke was small, about 135 pounds. If he had been a 200 pounder, he would have had to have been caged. David was one of the toughest smaller guys I ever coached. Too bad he and his cousin Nubbin could not have played on the team one year later. We would have been even better than we were.

Okemah High School Panthers—1969

Okemah Panthers

COACH: JOHN TATUM

ASSISTANT COACHES:
Jerry Johnston, John Adams & Roy Giles

PROBABLE STARTERS

OFFENSE

David King	(170)	sr.	22	Split End
Dal Campbell	(198)	jr.	70	Strongside Tackle
Terry Goode	(180)	sr.	60	Strongside Guard
Jim Bishop	(170)	jr.	50	Center
Dwayne Hibbs	(170)	jr.	65	Weakside Guard
Robert Ambrose	(170)	sr.	66	Weakside Tackle
Sam Palmer	(203)	sr.	80	Tight End
Ron Cottrell	(150)	jr.	10	Quarterback
Butch Standley	(170)	jr.	40	Fullback
Tom Rickner	(135)	jr.	20	Slot Back
John Martin	(180)	sr.	31	Tailback

DEFENSE

Lindall McLemore	(150)	sr.	41	Linebacker
Dennis Benson	(150)	soph.	32	Middle Linebacker
Bubby Ross	(150)	jr.	15	Halfback
Mike Aaron	(145)	soph.	11	Halfback

ALTERNATES

72-T Donald Denney (215) sr. 62-E Richard Collins (120) jr.
71-E Joe Fullbright (170) sr. 51-C Mike Brock (150) soph.
75-T Steve Howard (225) sr. 52-C Brian Cowan (135) soph.
 -T Fred Stephens (180) sr. 73-T Dave Fullbright (185) soph
42-B John Ward (125) sr. 74-E Wayne Lowery (130) soph.
61-B Dee Barton (125) jr. 67 G Kenney McLemore (145) soph.
63-E Jim Parks (145) jr.
82-E Charles Reeves (195) jr. 64-G Jerry Smith (140) soph.
83-E Bob Scully (125) soph. 84-B Larry Branscum (145) soph.
 G Mike Wilson (155) jr.

Okemah 1969 Football Team—Many years later…

A COACH'S IMPACT ON BOYS AND A COMMUNITY

One final story shows the impact a coach can have, not only on his players, but also on the entire community where he coaches. When asking for endorsements on this book, I asked one of my Okemah players, Mike Aaron, now practicing medicine in Weatherford, OK for his thoughts. Here is what Dr. Mike Aaron said...

THE DUST BOWL AND THE GREAT DEPRESSION LEFT A STIGMA THAT MANY associated with anyone from Oklahoma. This lasted long after the original events had occurred. The irony of that stigma was not lost on me that day when a new coach walked through the gates of an old WPA football stadium called the Pecan Bowl. John Tatum was a disciple of one of the greatest coaches of all time, Bud Wilkinson. I knew things were about to change, and they did.

No district championships in 15 years. Very few winning seasons faced this new coach. A culture of change came about because Coach Tatum would not accept mediocrity. He made us first believe in ourselves and then to believe in each other. He taught us to work hard. But he also taught us to respect others and to accept responsibility. We learned these things did not just apply to the football field but also to the classroom. His biology class was taught on a college level and certainly made my years of study much easier in college. I learned more about anatomy in his biology class than I did in my second year of medical school.

A district championship came along in 1969 and the first playoff game Okemah had experienced in many years. It started a tradition that endured long after both Coach Tatum and I left.

General Douglas Macarthur once said: "Sports keep alive in us a spirit and vitality. It teaches the strong to know when they are weak. The brave to face themselves when they are afraid. To be proud and bowed in defeat yet humble and gentle in victory. To learn to laugh, yet never forget how to weep. And to give the preponderance of courage over timidity."

John Tatum instilled these qualities in a bunch of eastern Oklahoma boys in need of someone to wipe the taste of the dust bowl stigma from their minds. Indeed he did this…and so much more.

Forty-five years later, those boys have aged. But to a man, each will tell you that those two years with John Tatum changed their lives for the better. In our minds we can still play the game we loved, even though our bodies would tell us otherwise. We all love John Tatum. Even though our time with him was brief, he changed our lives forever.

Dr. Mike Aaron and his wife, Jackie

ALL SPORTS BANQUET—COACH CHAIRBANKS

TO CLOSE THIS CHAPTER, HERE IS A TRUE STORY THAT COULD HAVE ONLY happened in a small town in central Oklahoma. Okemah, the small community with two water towers—one said Hot, the other said Cold! This story happened at the close of the second semester of school at Okemah. I had asked the superintendent when the All Sports banquet would be held.

The Superintendent was a tough old administrator named Cecil Oaks. He had been leading Okemah school systems since right before they had started putting air in footballs. They had never had an All Sports banquet before. So, I signed a contract saying that I would personally cover any and all expenses the banquet cost.

The first thing I did was call my old buddy and now assistant coach at OU, Leon Cross. I had Leon ask OU head football coach Chuck Fairbanks if he would come to Okemah and speak at our first ever banquet. Chuck agreed to speak after Leon told him that I had played at OU and was trying to build a football program at Okemah.

My newly formed and energized All Sports booster club and I sold tickets to attend the banquet, eat dinner, and hear the popular Coach Fairbanks speak. The tickets were a bargain—five bucks each. The fans of the Okemah football program were just unbelievable, always ready to help support the team in whatever way the program needed. Mack Smith was the tireless leader. Other Okemah boosters were eager to pitch in and help, folks like Jerry Smith, Tommy Duncan, Chubby Anderson, Bill Rickner, Nick Lambeth, Phil Standley, Bill Campbell, and Charley Elliott.

The event was held in the school gymnasium. It was an old gym with a raised stage at one end so we had a head table on the stage. Coach

Fairbanks, Tatum (the head football coach), and Charley Elliott, a local physician and president of the school board sat at the head table. Elliott was a good friend of Tatum and since he was also so well educated and good in front of a crowd, was the emcee for the evening. He sat next to Chuck Fairbanks. Of importance to this story is the fact that during the meal, Chuck accidentally ate Charley Elliott's peach cobbler.

It was soon time for Charley to introduce Chuck Fairbanks. So Charley, always the prepared one, had his notes and began to tell of Chuck's exploits like developing the Veer Offense as well as a myriad of other accomplishments as a coach. After two or three minutes of sharing the OU head coaches deeds, Charley closed his introduction thusly, "And now ladies and gentlemen, it is my pleasure to introduce the Head Football Coach of the University of Oklahoma, Coach F*ck Chairbanks!"

A collective gasp went up in the crowd of about 500 people. Being the head football coach, and seated on the stage, I acted like I had not heard the unbelievable gaff. Then, Tommy Duncan, a huge Okemah sports fan started laughing with a really loud bellowing laugh and the entire crowd joined in. The laugher must have lasted a good five minutes.

Chuck arose from his seat and Charley started toward his seat. The two men passed each other right behind my seat (Tatum) and I heard Charley say to Chuck, "That will teach you to eat my peach cobbler!"

To this day, I am not certain whether Charley's introduction was the gaff of all times or if it was the all times, "that will teach you to eat my pie" barb.

Leon Cross later added this…at the Monday morning OU football coaching staff meeting, Chuck Fairbanks said this, "Men, you won't believe what happened to me this weekend at Okemah…"

At the end of Fairbanks' talk, he did something that truly underscored what a class act he was. He closed his speech by complimenting me on the great job of rebuilding Okemah's football program. And he then said, "I usually charge 300 dollars plus my travel expenses to speak at functions like this. But tonight, please put that money into Tatum's football budget so he will have some extra money for his program."

And that was an act of kindness that made me a real Chuck Fairbanks fan.

OU Head Football Coach—Chuck Fairbanks

LEAVING THE JOB I LOVED

A FEW DAYS AFTER THE DISAPPOINTING LOSS IN THE PLAYOFFS, AN ARTERY ruptured in my nose. I thought I was going to bleed to death. Doc Elliott could not get it stopped. I bled off and on for five days. Finally, Charley sent me to the hospital in Tulsa and in surgery an ENT specialist put a posterior nose pack in to stop the bleeding. Four days later after he had removed the pack and successfully stopped the bleeding, I asked him what caused it? He told me it was stress. He asked me what I did for a living. I told him I was a high school football coach. He suggested I find another way to make a living.

Epilog on Okemah: As great a year as '69 had been, I knew I had to try to move on. I was now a veteran coach with a good track record. I heard the Miami, Oklahoma head coaching job was open. I wrote a letter to the Miami board of education and applied for the job. Later I heard over 200 coaches had applied. The board cut the applicants to a final ten and interviewed them. I was one of the ten.

I drove up to Miami for my interview. The board cut the ten to the top three, and I was one of the top three and went back for a second interview. About five days later I got a call from the Miami Superintendent of Schools. He told me, "John, we had a really tough decision and decided to hire a coach who is an assistant coach at a university. Just so you know, you were the only high school coach we interviewed in the top three…the other two are college assistant coaches. Then the Superintendent thanked me for my interest in Miami High School, I thanked him for the consideration, and the call ended.

It was about ten days or so later that my phone rang. It was the Miami Superintendent of Schools. He said, "John, the University will not release from his contract their assistant coach we wanted to hire, so we would like to offer you the head coaching position." I thanked him and told him I was not interested. I could tell even over the phone that he was stunned. "Why," he asked, "I thought you really wanted this job."

I told him I did and went on to explain. I told him that never in my life had I ever settled for second place and I was not going to start with Miami. I was not their first choice and would not be their second choice either. I thanked the Superintendent and the call ended. It was a difficult choice to make but my principles were at stake and I would not compromise them, no matter what.

And I "walked the walk." Six weeks later I would leave high school teaching and coaching and enter the insurance business. I ended up as the CEO running a multi-billion dollar company. Things really do work out for the best if you just believe they will. I would never coach again.

To show their gratitude for the job I had done for them, the Okemah school board gave me a $300 a year raise—a whopping 25 dollars a month. I taught three biology classes and a general science class, was the head football coach and head track coach. I was paid $7900 a year, and I had six years of teaching experience and a Master's Degree. Every year I plunged more deeply in debt. We owed everyone in town…even the blood bank!

I didn't know what I was going to do but I had to do something. So I left the life I loved, coaching young men, and went into a business I knew absolutely nothing about—selling insurance. When I handed the superintendent of schools at Okemah my resignation, he read it and asked me to give him one good reason why I was doing this. I looked him straight in the eye and said, "Okay Bob, how about this reason…You do not deserve someone with the kind of talent and ability I have." I had to make it outside of teaching for I had not just burned my bridges…I had dynamited them.

A few days later a television crew from Tulsa came to Okemah to interview me for the 10 o'clock sports. The last question the sports reporter asked me was, "What are you going to do now, Coach Tatum?"

I told him, "I do not know except for this…I can tell you two things I am not going to do...I will never coach again and I am not going to sell insurance." In retrospect...hey, I was half right.

My wife at the time told me, "I don't know what you think you can do. All you know anything about is coaching." How about that for a strong vote of confidence? Charlie Elliott, a local doctor and president of the Okemah school board kept telling me I was wasting my time coaching and teaching. He is the one who first told me I could do anything I wanted to do.

I knew this, I would walk into a sporting goods store with Charlie and he could pick up a gun, or a rod and reel, or a new shirt, and buy any of them without even asking what it cost. I had never been around anyone like that before. He could also order a fine steak and have a couple of martini's and not think a thing about spending 40 bucks for a good meal in a really nice restaurant. It was a life style I would like to try living—it looked fun and exciting.

I struggled to decide whether to leave the vocation I loved...coaching young people. Finally, I relied on something my great Uncle Albert had once told me. "You can't steal second with your foot on first." It was time for me to run the bases. And I did. My great friend Charles Elliott kept telling me that I was smart, talented, and wasting my abilities. He was like another Port Robertson. I was about to leave a career I genuinely loved to sell insurance. I was about to try to steal second base.

I am including this chapter because our high schools are the building grounds for our college athletes and, even more importantly, the work force for future America. We must have great teachers who not only teach but also mold the minds of our future countrymen. Our teachers deserve to be highly compensated. It is too bad that our Oklahoma teachers rank about #25 nationally in compensation.

As a former CEO of a large regional company I knew this...if as a company we paid peanuts, we got monkeys. Our compensation levels allowed my company to attract some of the very best business leaders of the area. And consequently, we were a leader in the industry we competed for business within. If we want top-notch educators, we must, as citizens, be willing to support the competitive environment that will attract the very best educators. It is really just that simple.

I left teaching and the coaching that I loved. I missed working with the kids at Okemah and Star Spencer. It was very rewarding to teach the skills which I had learned from my college coaches at OU. I also learned a great deal from the coaching clinics that I attended. But in the end, the business world offered great challenges for me. My business career was the kind of challenge Port would have been proud of my accepting. It forced me to use all my ability and, because of those challenges, I loved to get up every day and go to work.

I learned that being a CEO (Chief Executive Officer) is a whole lot like coaching and teaching. In a real sense of the word, I never really left teaching and coaching. I was truly blessed to have been able to work with so many great athletes and employees. The lessons I had learned as an athlete, and as a coach, and at Star Spencer and Okemah had prepared me to be successful in business.

At each and every new challenge given to me in business, I set my goals extremely high, used all the advice my mentors had given me, and excelled at the new challenges. Sports and my coaches and teachers had taught me well. Both Port and Charles Elliott were right, and along with my Uncle Albert, they convinced me to take a chance. Accept the risk, play your heart out and find the pot of gold at the end of the rainbow (dream). The three changed my life forever.

MY HEAVENER HIGH SCHOOL TEAMMATES—AN EXCEPTIONAL GROUP OF GUYS

I HAVE, FOR MOST OF MY LIFE, FELT THAT MOST AWARDS AND HONORS ARE overblown. In my case, whatever honor came my way is more of a reflection of my teammates than anything I was credited for doing. My high school teammates at Heavener High School were truly an exceptional bunch of athletes.

The photo showing the HHS offensive team of 1958 from left to right with the line first is, RE Ronald Bennett, RT Glen Lazalier, RG Don Huie, C Bud Thompson, LG Larry Pyles, LT Robert Rockman, LE Don Frost, and the backfield, left to right...Right HB Jim Davis, Fullback John Tatum, Quarterback Hal Dowden, and Left HB Roger Webb. It should be noted that during the fifth game of the 1958 HS football season, our center, Bud Thompson suffered a season ending injury. His replacement was Bob Babcock, a sophomore, who played center with the other 10 starters who were seniors. Jerry Johnston, also a sophomore, replaced Bob on defense—the rest of the team played both offense and defense.

Heavener High School, a small railroad town nestled in the foothills of the Ozarks, had a population of about 2500 people. In Oklahoma High School football rankings we were class B in a system that the largest High Schools in Oklahoma were AA, then A, then B, then C.

My classmates and teammates were indeed exceptional. Our football team had 11 seniors and two sophomores who played in games. Out of 13 players, 9 went on to college and graduated. Three had advanced degrees. Four were coaches and/or teachers. Roger Webb became the President of Central Oklahoma State University. Glen Lazalier earned an advanced degree in Physics and was the lead Physicist over roughly

600 engineers in the Defense industry. Hal Dowden rose to the very top in football officiating, becoming a referee in the Big XII conference. Jim Davis joined the USMC and became a pilot serving as a Marine Corp Helicopter Pilot and doing two hitches in Vietnam. After a second tour in Nam, Davis was assigned to the USS Nimitz aircraft carrier where he flew the A-6 Fixed wing jet fighter plane. After a lifetime career in the USMC, Major Jim Davis retired.

Bud Thompson, our center who was hurt in mid-season, was our High School class president and spent over 30 years working in Dallas for Texas Instruments. Sadly, he died in May 2014. Don Huie taught art at Poteau and Heavener High Schools and also died too soon. Robert Rockman is a licensed mortician who went on to the Oklahoma State Health Department, a career he retired from. Larry Pyles graduated from college, spent three years in the Army, five years with IBM, and thirty years with Amoco, with twenty of those years in management. His favorite job title is Dad.

Our two co-captains were Don Frost and Ron Bennett…two of the toughest players to ever crap between two shoes. Frost graduated from college, returned to Heavener and taught school at his alma mater. In his spare time, he built a small but lucrative chicken business. He and his wife, Lucretia, are the only teammates that still reside in Heavener. Ron Bennett went from High School to the US Army where he became a medic, stationed in Germany. He returned to work for Texas Power and Light Company, using his GI bill to take a course in power line construction and management. Bennett worked his way up the line and retired as the Superintendent for Texas Utilities and Fuel Company. When Bennett retired he was third in line to the Vice President of the company.

And finally, John Tatum, spent 34 years in the insurance industry, retiring in 2004 as the Executive Vice President and General Manager of Farm Bureau Mutual Insurance Company. The company sold all lines of insurance in Iowa, South Dakota, Minnesota, Utah, Nebraska, Kansas, Arizona, and New Mexico. After retiring from his position as Senior VP and CEO of Farm Bureau Mutual, Tatum turned to writing. His first book, The *Sooner The Better* was followed by this book, *Sooner Football: Old School and other Interesting Stories*.

What about the two sophomores who managed to break into the lineup...Bob Babcock and Jerry Johnston? Johnston became a football coach, winning the State Championship at a couple of different Oklahoma High Schools and was inducted into the Oklahoma High School Coaches Hall of Fame. My childhood friend, Bob Babcock, served as a rifle platoon leader in Vietnam, retired from an executive career at IBM, started Deeds Publishing Company (publisher of this and my first book), and is heavily involved in organizations related to veterans of the US military services.

Heavener High School starting team—1958
Line (L to R) Will Bennett, Glen Lazalier, Don Huie, Bud Thompson, Larry Pyles, Robert Rockeman, Don Frost
Backs (L to R) Jim Davis, John Tatum, Hal Dowden, Roger Webb

CARL TWIDWELL, MY HIGH SCHOOL COACH

I CANNOT REMEMBER THE EXACT YEAR COACH TWIDWELL ARRIVED IN Heavener, Oklahoma. Maybe it was 1953 or 1954. I was in the eighth grade and became the water boy. Twidwell would become the major male influence in my life. My father had abandoned my mother, older sister, and me in 1947.

It would prove to be one of the significant turning points in my young life. Coach Twidwell became sort of my father by proxy. He influenced me to become an athlete.

It is well documented on how I became a center, but not so much how I came to be a fullback. Going into our senior year, Twidwell lined up the entire team of what would be the 1958 Heavener football team and had a race of about 50 or 60 yards. The four fastest runners would become the backfield that fall.

The fastest four Heavener runners were Roger Webb, who had been a second team guard the year before. Jim Davis, who had been the starting quarterback the year before. Hal Dowden, who had been a second team end the year before. And John Tatum, who had been the starting center the year before. Coach Twidwell then moved Dowden to quarterback, Webb to left halfback, Davis to right halfback, and Tatum to fullback.

At the OU coaching clinic, Twidwell spoke with Coach Wilkinson, asking him about the move of Tatum from center to fullback and would that hurt Tatum's chances for a scholarship to college. (See the scanned letter from Wilkinson to Tatum on page xxv.)

HHS went on to post a great football season, thanks to 11 great seniors and two great sophomores. Twidwell graduated with us seniors and moved to a new high school in Oklahoma City, Star Spencer High School where he succeeded in building a great high school football program.

Twidwell was elected to the Oklahoma Football Coaches Hall of Fame and the football field at Star Spencer is Twidwell Field.

San Toi DeBose, Oklahoma Back of the Year in 1964 from Star-Spencer High School, Coach Carl Twidwell, and John Tatum

A FEW MORE MEMORIES FROM HHS

EACH SPRING AT OU ONE OF THE HIGHLIGHTS IS THE RED/WHITE SPRING game. The weekend is packed with events for former OU lettermen from all varsity sports...both men and women letter winners. This past spring (April of 2015) at a cocktail party held for past letter winners, old JET turned around and there was one of the most influential men in the history of Oklahoma University, former OU Regent Jack Santee of Tulsa. I had heard a great many stories about so many decisions the Board of Regents and especially Jack Santee had made which positively affected the University so I was very anxious to be presented with the opportunity to meet this hero of mine.

I stood next to Jack and waited for him to finish a conversation with another admirer. Finally Jack turned to face me and I said, "Jack, you don't know me but I am John Tatum."

Jack then interrupted me saying, "I know who you are, John, and furthermore, I have known you for a very long time." I couldn't imagine how or even where we could have met before, so I asked where we had met.

Jack paused for a moment then replied, "John I first was acquainted with you in September of 1958 when you led a bunch of hillbillies to Tulsa and gave my Tulsa Marquette football team a good old fashioned butt kicking to open the 1958 High school football season."

I nodded and politely said, "As I recall the country kids were 48 and the big city kids were 7." I didn't remember that Jack Santee was ever a coach. I thought he was a great lawyer and outstanding Regent...and still regard him as such.

The Heavener Wolves had a super season in 1958. We won the old Black

Diamond Conference Championship and placed six players on the All Conference team. One of the unrealized highlights would not occur until several years later in a land far away called Nam...as in Vietnam. The Heavener Wolves met the Okmulgee Dunbar Tigers on Thanksgiving day at 2:00 pm in the Oklahoma class B football semi-final game.

The game turned out to be the last for my Wolves, Okmulgee Dunbar beat us 26-6 on a cold Thanksgiving day. But years later, it would become a very significant event and rate as most memorable to all the players on both teams, for in our midst that day was a bona fide American Hero, an Okmulgee substitute that did not play much. His name is Melvin Morris.

Mr. Melvin Morris was the recipient of the United States of America's highest award—the Medal of Honor. Long past the time it was due, in March 2014, Staff Sergeant Melvin Morris received from President Barack Obama the Medal of Honor in a ceremony at the White House honoring 24 American heroes who had been overlooked in the past.

Soon after graduating from high school, Melvin Morris joined the Army and was one of the first class of Green Berets, established by President John F. Kennedy. His Medal of Honor citation reads:

For conspicuous gallantry and intrepidity at the risk of his life above and beyond the call of duty:

"Staff Sergeant Melvin Morris distinguished himself by acts of gallantry and intrepidity above and beyond the call of duty while serving as Commander of a Strike Force drawn from Company D, 5th Special Forces Group (Airborne), 1st Special Forces, during combat operations against an armed enemy in the vicinity of Chi Lang, Republic of Vietnam on September 17, 1969. On that afternoon, Staff Sergeant Morris' affiliated companies encountered an extensive enemy mine field and were subsequently engaged by a hostile force. Staff Sergeant Morris learned by radio that a fellow team commander had been killed near an enemy bunker and he immediately reorganized his men into an effective assault posture before advancing forward and splitting off with two men to recover the team commander's body. Observing the maneuver, the hostile force concentrated its fire on Staff Sergeant Morris' three-man element and successfully wounded both men accompanying him. After assisting the two wounded men back to his forces' lines, Staff Sergeant Morris charged forward into withering enemy fire with only his men's suppressive fire as cover. While enemy machine gun emplacements continuously directed strafing fusillades against him, Staff Sergeant Morris destroyed the positions with hand grenades and continued his assault, ultimately eliminating four bunkers. Upon reaching the bunker nearest the fallen team commander, Staff Sergeant Morris repulsed the enemy, retrieved his comrade and began the arduous trek back to friendly lines. He was wounded three times as he struggled forward, but ultimately succeeded in returning his fallen comrade to a friendly position. Staff Sergeant Morris' extraordinary heroism and selflessness above and beyond the call of duty are in keeping with the highest traditions of military service and reflect great credit upon himself, his unit, and the United States Army.

A football game on a cold, snowy Thanksgiving afternoon in Heavener, Oklahoma pales in comparison to what Melvin Morris accomplished so long ago in Vietnam. Thankfully, he is still alive and was at the White House to receive his well-earned Medal of Honor in the White House ceremony. Some day I hope to be able to shake his hand.

When I look back upon the 1958 football season I have but one regret, that Heavener didn't defeat Okmulgee and Bixby did not defeat Grove. For had they both won, Heavener and Bixby, the Heavener Flash would have had the opportunity to knock my future roommate, the Phantom, into next week in the state football playoffs. What a hoot that would have been. In retrospect, it would have been a chance for me to get even with John Porterfield for him sending me off to class with two socks that did not match.

JOHN TATUM

Dan George, Inc.
Attorney at Law

Telephone 918-775-5515
Home 918-775-4870
Fax 918-775-3271

P.O. Box 748
1015 E. Redwood
Sallisaw, Oklahoma 74955

Memo

Thursday, September 02, 2010

Dear John

Sometime back I heard you were living in Eufaula. The article in the Indian Journal was most interesting and of course I had to have your book. I also bought a copy for our good friend Jimmy Payne---we were in law school together. The books came in today.

Our senior year at Eufaula we changed conferences. I remember wondering where Heavener was. Back then we did not scout the other team, certainly one not as far away as Heavener----so we didn't know what we were in for until we saw ya'll in warm up and heard the pre-game pep talk. It was brief and to the point.

"Boys just to the best you can and try not to get hurt".

The ball would snap and puff----our line from tackle to tackle would vanish, (linebackers also) and here you would come. I would grab a hold (all 135 lb.) and hang on until helped arrived----provided you didn't swat me off before hand. After a quarter or so of this humiliation I vowed to bring down your big ass solo.

Next snap, same story, and here you came. Maybe it was just me but you never seemed to try any evasive maneuvering. This time I went straight at you. Upon awaking I was surprised to see you down also. I think your cleats got tangled up in my flesh and you tripped because I was skinned from the waist up.

To hell with this and I went back to hanging on. I thought the score was 40 zip but I just spoke with Doug Hopkins, retired chemist who lives in Eufaula also, and he said the score was 58 zip. He was about my size and played center and said there was this line backer who he never could block and gave him a bloody nose to boot. Guess you did damage both ways.

Doug and I would be honored to buy you a chicken fried steak at JMs. We can remember when they were 35 cents and Pepsi a dime. There is no need to wonder what we look like because we will recognize you. Give me call if you can.

I received this letter from a guy we had played against my senior season…

184

SOME FINAL TIDBITS TO WRAP UP THE HIGH SCHOOL SECTION

OKIES: I HAVE LIVED ABOUT HALF OF MY LIFE IN THE GREAT STATE OF NAtive America...Okla "by god" Homa as the natives like to say. Oklahoma's favorite son, Will Rogers said it best, "I never met a man I didn't like." Rephrased it would be this way, "I have not met many Okies I did not like." Following are some of the best Okie stories I can recall.

I coached at Star Spencer with a great guy named Dave Selph. Dave and I had both grown up in Heavener. Dave was about four years older than me, sort of a hero I looked up to. We were getting ready to play Bishop Mc Guiness in football one year. McGuiness had a great team and we had only two chances to beat them, Slim and None. Dave volunteered to go over and scout them in practice. We fixed up Dave's car to look like he was transporting boxes, which were a rue to hide him under.

The boxes had a slit in them so he could look out with field glasses and chart plays. Dave and I had it all figured out, except for the weather. We did not factor in the 100-degree day. The heat almost got old Dave. He had to abandon his subcompact station wagon and go to a chain link fence, part the ivy and take a peak at the Bishop McGuiness football powerhouse.

All of a sudden Dave heard a door open from the backside of a furniture store. Quickly and with all of the cool of a Mississippi river boat gambler, Dave pivoted and aimed the binoculars up into a giant elm tree nearby. The man emerging from the store asked if he had a squirrel treed. Dave turned to the guy and proclaimed, "No Sir, I am a bird watcher."

Dave returned with a scouting report...McGuiness had a big tight end and they were faking to their fullback inside and hitting the tight end deep over the middle. I had scouted McGuiness and knew for a fact they did not have a big tight end.

Game time came and about the fourth play of McGuiness's offensive possession, they faked to their fullback inside and threw a long pass over the middle to a big tight end. They had moved their fullback to tight end!

I learned a very important lesson…listen carefully to your scouting report. It would not have mattered because McGuiness drew and quartered us that night on the gridiron.

My last year of coaching came in 1969 at Okemah. They were not known for their high school football powers. My first year at Okemah, we won four games and I could have been elected mayor. By Okemah standards, it was a great year.

I was disappointed but optimistic. I had some great kids coming back and super support in the community. I started a class for mothers and girl friends. I called it Football 101. I taught the ladies of Okemah how to watch and understand the game of football.

Many of my players were Creek Indians and were the greatest kids to coach I was ever around. We were playing Bristow, at Bristow, and had just completed our pregame warm up. We were headed toward the locker room for pregame bathroom stops and such. On the way to the locker room, our tailback, John Martin, who also did our kickoffs came up to me and informed me that Dwayne Hibbs, our starting guard, had accidentally run into him and gave him a charley horse in the thigh of his kicking leg. He could not kick off. To make matters "ever worser" as Port Robertson used to say at OU, we had just lost the toss and were to kick off to start the game.

We got into the dressing room and I asked for everyone's attention. I explained that John Martin cannot kickoff and asked for a volunteer. Nobody stepped forward. So I had another go at the situation. "Look, we lost the toss and have to kick off, now I need someone to step forward and volunteer to kickoff."

David King raised his hand. He was a senior and one of my all time favorite players. He is a 6"2" Creek, our starting split end. He could run and jump and was very confident. I reaffirmed David's commitment to kickoff.

We were headed onto the field and David came running over to me and said, "Coach, how do I kick off?"

I explained to David, "You take the ball, put it on the tee, jack around with it and act like you know what you are doing, pace off ten yards, then when the referee blows his whistle, run up there and kick the crap out of it."

David teed up the ball. The ref blew his whistle and David started running toward his teed up target, the football.

When he got to the ball he planted his right foot and swung his left leg toward the football. He almost completely missed the ball, hitting it about two or three inches from the top. The ball spun off the tee and spinned downfield about 12 yards. Our scat back, Tommy RIckner, a championship sprinter, ran down field and covered the ball. The "Onside Kick" to open the game caught Bristow totally off guard and led the way for an upset win of their favored team.

After the game, a sports reporter from the Tulsa World newspaper was interviewing me. He said, "Coach, the onside kick caught Bristow completely off guard. I don't believe I have ever seen a team onside kick off the opening kickoff."

I replied, "Well we had an excellent scouting report on Bristow's kickoff return team and felt it was a good call for us to start the game and change their teams confidence." I just didn't have the guts to tell the reporter that David just about missed the ball and the onside kick was a fluke and we were lucky to have covered the ball.

Sometimes it is better to be lucky than good. And my Okemah Panthers were playing Bristow with Lady Luck on their shoulders.

SECTION THREE
Other Interesting Stories Worth Telling

SOONER MAGIC WOMEN

OLD JET IS NOT JUST AN OU FOOTBALL FAN. OH NO, WOMEN'S SPORTS ARE a personal favorite. Turn the pages back in time and Peggy Llewellyn Tatum was a huge influence on young Mr. JET. She was JET's three-year older sister. Lou, as she was known, was born about 50 some odd years too early. Had she been born in the past 30 years or so, hands down, she would have won Olympic Gold in the hammer throw or the shot put or discus.

No doubt about it, sister Lou was one tough cookie. She could whip her little brother's ass in a New York minute. In fact, brother JET couldn't get the best of big sister until he was about 25 years old.

When Lou was a senior in high school, her class went on a senior trip to Rockaway Beach, Missouri. The destination was a big amusement park. One of the attractions was a punching bag that measured how much force one could hit the bag with a punch.

The boys all goaded Lou to hit the bag. After several minutes of pleading with her to throw her best punch, she finally did. She literally knocked the bag off the chain.

I always knew there was a place in athletics for women. I was thrilled when OU opened up athletic programs in gymnastics, softball, soccer, rowing, track, and basketball for college women. I have followed those programs faithfully, especially OU women's gymnastics, softball, and basketball.

All the women's coaches are excellent, but my favorite two coaches are Patty Gasso and Sherri Coale. I believe those two are exceptional coaches in their programs. And when it comes to Sooner Magic, a couple of years back, we were treated to one of the very best Sooner Magic moments of all time and of all sports.

The Sooner Magic Moment occurred in the first game of the finals of women's softball for the national championship. The first game of the best-two-out-of-three series was in extra innings. Tennessee was at bat in the top half of extra innings, the score 0-0. The Vols had two runners on base when their hitter hit a home run over the right-center field. The Sooner outlook was dismal to say the very least. The Vols led OU 3-0 with the Sooners coming to bat in the bottom of the extra inning.

The Sooners had the bottom of their lineup hitting, and for 12 innings had been scoreless. But alas, Gasso's crew wasn't dead just yet, a series of doubles and the Sooners closed the gap and a homerun tied the game 3-3. The Sooner defense held and in the bottom of the 13th inning, Lauren Chamberlain, the Babe Ruth of college softball, hit a homerun with a Sooner runner on first and the Lady Sooner's won the game. It was truly Sooner Magic.

The Lady Sooners smoked the Vols in the second game and Patty Gasso's team won her second National Championship at OU. The first game will go down in history as Sooner Magic of the highest order, truly a magnificent moment in Sooner sports history.

I was both happy and sad…happy that I had witnessed a great comeback win for Patty Gasso's softball team, but sad thinking about my sister and how there was little to no opportunity for women in sports back in the day when she could have been a star in softball or basketball or track.

The OU basketball program is every bit as exceptional as OU men's sports. Old JET really got interested in OU women's basketball several years ago when the Lady Sooners round ballers had a player, Caton Hill, that wore number 12. What made her so much fun to watch was that her daddy, Bill Hill, the one and only Marlow Flash, was old JET's teammate on the OU football team in the early 60s.

Caton went on to graduate from OU and became a physician. She now serves as a captain in the US Army medical corps in San Antonio, Texas.

Back to Sooner round ball. Sherri Coale is a great coach. She came up through the high school ranks and is considered an elite coach in her profession. I love to watch her teams play. They are relentless and I am so proud of the class and distinction the Lady Sooners play with...it is for sure a reflection of their coach.

Like Patty Gasso, Sherri Coale is a winner in every respect. It is too bad my sister Lou could not have been a part of one of those excellent athletic programs. Of course I am prejudiced but I am a fair judge of athletic talent, and my sister Lou was big and strong, had great hand eye coordination, and could run fast. On top of all that, she was brave and daring. Don't forget tough either...and toughness she possessed in spades! When we were kids in the neighborhood playing a game of football, my sister Lou was always the first player chosen! And she was the only girl in the game, too.

OU WRESTLING—MARK TATUM

MARCH 21, 1965...THE DAY MY FIRST SON WAS BORN AT BAPTIST HOSPITAL in Oklahoma City, Oklahoma. John Mark Tatum, from the get-go, was an adventure. Let's fast-forward several years in young Mr. Tatum's life. Throughout the years, Mark displayed an incredible resolve to conquer challenges. He was relentless when confronted by a new physical activity like learning to ride a bicycle. In no time at all, he wanted the training wheels off the new bike...like on the second day! In a few weeks, he was jumping barbed wire fences.

It was the same with skateboards or learning to do half gainers off a low diving board. As his father, I learned to say this to Mark at a very early age when he would ask me about taking up any new challenge, "If you work hard enough at this goal you have Mark, well you can do it." And off he would go, hell bent on learning to master the new physical challenge.

One of the physical gifts that Mark was born with was he could use either arm and hand with equal efficiency...he was ambidextrous. When he wanted to learn to play tennis, he refused to learn to hit a back hand shot, he would simply switch the racquet to whichever hand the ball was approaching and return it with a forehand shot. Being ambidextrous would prove to be a tremendous advantage in different sports, like golf and wrestling.

Mark was a naturally aggressive boy. It is no wonder that he was drawn toward the sport of wrestling. When Mark was a sophomore at Ponca City High School, he informed me that he was going to win the Oklahoma State Championship in his weight class. I responded with my usual answer to Mark, "Well, you can if you work hard enough at mastering the basic fundamentals."

After his junior year, he informed me that he was going to attend college on a wrestling scholarship. By the end of his senior year, he was the Oklahoma State Champion at 191 pounds and the number one ranked free style wrestler in the nation at 190 pounds. His dream was to wrestle for Dan Gable and the Iowa Hawkeyes. But for some reason, Gable would not recruit Mark. That decision would come back to bite Dan Gable and his Iowa program.

In the absence of a scholarship offer from Iowa, Mark chose to follow his Dad and sign with the Oklahoma Sooners. The head wrestling coach at OU was the legendary two time National Champion Stan Abel. Abel and old JET were athletes at OU at the same time and knew each other well. Stan Abel would prove to be probably the only wrestling coach in the college ranks that could handle Mark. Coach Abel was one of the toughest wrestlers Port Robertson had ever recruited to wrestle for OU. Stan Abel became a great wrestling technician. His wrestlers, including Mark Tatum, were excellent wrestlers and formidable opponents on the mat.

Coach Abel recounted several Mark Tatum stories. Abel recruited many of the nation's top heavyweight wrestlers so that Mark Tatum would have a workout partner. Abel also wanted those heavies to learn from Tatum and become better wrestlers. But Tatum had a different idea about why Stan kept recruiting heavyweights. Mark thought Stan was trying to replace him. So, in the course of working out, Tatum would actually and literally torture the incoming heavyweights to the point where virtually all of them would eventually quit.

Finally, Stan Abel recruited a world-beater from Illinois—a state champion heavyweight from a state known for producing great wrestlers. One day in practice, one of the wrestlers came running up to Stan and said, "Mark Tatum is beating up the freshman from Illinois, Coach."

Coach Abel, ran over to the heavyweight mat and the two behemoths were going at it. Abel quickly put a halt to it saying, "You two stop it. You are supposed to be helping each other, now shake hands and get back to wrestling drills." So the two heavies shook hands.

Stan turned and started to walk away. A ruckus erupted and Stan turned to find Mark beating on the Illinois star heavyweight again. Abel yelled at Tatum, "Alright that does it, Tatum, get out of here."

Tatum turned to face his Coach, staring defiantly and said, "You are going to have to call security to get me out of here."

Stan Abel started laughing and said, "So alright, let's get back to wrestling."

In a few weeks, the Illinois high school star surrendered and went back to Illinois.

Mark's coach credits Mark with winning a couple of Big 8 championships. One of those championships came down to a heavyweight match between Tatum and the super large Nebraska heavyweight, Gary Albright. Albright was about 6'5" and weighed in at something north of 350 pounds. Mark was about 250 pounds, giving away 100 pounds to Albright. Mark beat Albright in overtime and on criteria giving OU the conference championship.

Another big match for Mark Tatum came in the quarterfinals on the National Championships held in Iowa City, Iowa. Mark was wrestling a big tall heavyweight from Iowa named Sidlinger, who also played tackle on the Iowa football team. Mark upset the Iowa wrestler. That loss cost Iowa and its coach, Dan Gable, his 10th straight National Championship. After the referee had raised Mark's arm as the match winner, Mark walked over to the storied Iowa coach and said to him, "See Coach, I told you that you should have recruited me out of high school!"

Gable nodded in agreement and replied to Mark, "You're right, Mark, I should have."

The greatest matches were the Bedlam matches between the Sooners and Aggies of Oklahoma A&M aka...OSU. One memorable match was Mark's senior year in a dual meet with the Aggies at Stillwater. Mark was literally torturing the OSU heavyweight. The OSU wrestler was moaning as Mark Tatum tightened his painful hold on him. Then Tatum let him up and immediately took the Aggie down again, putting him right back in the same painful hold. Again the OSU wrestler would grimace and groan because of the intense pain. Tatum reveled in torturing the OSU wrestler. When the match ended and the ref raised Tatum's arm in victory, Tatum shot the entire crowd at Galleger Iba arena the "You're number one" sign! The crowd booed Tatum in unison.

The final hoorah for Mark Tatum his last year of eligibility came at the National Championship matches held at Ames, Iowa in 1988. Mark was a 5th year senior and was to wrestle in the consolation finals against Joel Greenlee. Greenlee was wrestling for Northern Iowa University. He would become the Heavyweight National Champion the following year…1989. But in '88 he would wrestle the mauler from OU, Mark Tatum. Mark was leading 5-3 late in the third period when Greenlee reversed Tatum and the two went out of bounds. Now the score was tied 5-5 with 12 seconds remaining in the match with Tatum in the down position.

The referee blew the whistle and Mark Tatum executed a perfect Gramby Roll, an escape move more likely used by smaller and more agile wrestlers, and Mark escaped Greenlee's grasp with seven seconds remaining in the match. Tatum won the match 6-5 and became an All-American, thus achieving his final goal as a college athlete.

Stan Abel credits Mark with being one of his favorite wrestlers. Abel said of Tatum, "Mark was a very intense wrestler…one of the most intense that I ever coached." Abel continued his praise of Mark, "and Tatum was one of the most likeable wrestlers too, he had a lot of charisma. It was hard for anyone to not like Mark, he was just fun to be around."

Tatum wrestled with a group of talented wrestlers. They became lifelong friends with Mark—Rod Thornton, TJ Sewal, Carl Sewal, Junior Meeks, Kenny Fischer, Daron Babcock, Dan Chaid, Joe Reynolds, Toni Bellai, and Joe Stafford. The group gets together from time to time to relive that time when their testosterone was out of control.

One year, Kenny Fischer, Junior Meeks, and Daron Babcock lived together in what became known as "the wrestling house." One week-end after wrestling season was over, the wrestlers threw a "Kegger." Several athletes attended as all present kicked in a few bucks to pay for the sarsaparilla in the keg of Bud. Daron Babcock had obtained a free keg from his future father in law, former OU track star Bob Knight. Daron was the bartender and sold the free beer to the athletes in attendance.

One of the athletes in attendance was a future NFL Buffalo Bill football player, Jerry Craft. Craft, in a rambunctious moment, accidentally broke a window. The wrestlers demanded that Craft pay for it. He refused but kept partaking of the keg. Jerry Craft was 6'5" and weighed 343 pounds. None of the wrestlers in attendance were willing to try to collect from the big guy so they did the smart thing…they waited on their big guy to show up, heavyweight Mark Tatum.

When he arrived, Kenny Fischer, Junior Meeks, and Daron Babcock had a meeting with Mark explaining how Craft had broken a window and refused to pay for it. According to Babcock, Kenny Fischer and all 150 pounds of him picked up Craft and carried him to the front door and threw him outside. That is where Tatum approached the titan tackle and said, "You broke the window and you are going to pay for it." Craft had some X rated comment which translated meant, "I am not paying and you cannot make me."

In a move which called on Tatum's catlike quickness, and faster than a hiccup, Craft went crashing to the floor. Craft had forgotten Port's advice; don't mess with the wrestlers! After a complete beating administered by Tatum, Jerry Craft said, "Why don't I pay for the window and lets all get back to sipping sarsaparilla!" And they did.

When word got back to Craft's football coach, the legendary one… the King…Barry Switzer, the football coach asked Mark to quit beating up his football players. And for the record, so did the men's basketball coaches.

In March of 1987, Mark Tatum wrestled in a Sombo tournament with the Oklahoma Under Dogs team and won the National Championship for the 220+ pound weight class. In November of '87, Mark was notified that he would be representing the USA in the World Sombo Championships in Milan, Italy. Mark represented the USA in the heavyweight class

JOHN TATUM

of 220+ pound wrestlers, wrestling at about 265 pounds. He acquitted himself nicely, coming away with the Bronze Medal, finishing behind the Champion, a Russian, and a second place Bulgarian.

Tatum's third place finish was what many believe was the first medal finish by an American Sombo style wrestler. Sombo style wrestling is patterned after the hand to hand combat systems of the Russian and Chinese military. Wrestlers can utilize submission holds and if their opponent does not "tap out," their arm or leg can be broken and thus end the match.

Sombo style is very similar to modern cage fighting except there is no punching in Sombo. In addition, Mark Tatum also entered a Judo tourney and won the heavyweight division, having never before seen a judo event.

Mark wrestled in the waning moments of a collegiate unlimited weight class for the heavyweight division. Mark Tatum had won the state championship at 190 pounds in high school. 190 was his natural weight class, but at OU Dan Chaid was a returning All American and would go on to win a National Championship at that weight class. If Tatum wanted to wrestle, it was either go down a weight class or up a weight class. He chose to go up, and as a heavyweight he would often be outweighed by as much as 100 pounds. His last two years, the NCAA put a weight class limit on the heavyweights of 285. That rule change by the NCAA made the heavyweight class more competitive and even more importantly, healthier for the athletes.

Had this weight class change been enacted years earlier, Mark Tatum would have had a much better won/loss record for sure. But in the first years at OU, Tatum gave up just too much weight. Gary Albright was so large, the OU wrestlers called him the USS Albright…because he was large like a battleship! I do not recall his name, but Iowa State had a heavyweight larger than the USS Albright. Never the less, in 1988, Mark Tatum finished tied for 7th place all time for Pins at OU. Another interesting fact for the time period Tatum wrestled at OU was the lineup for dual meets. The smallest weight wrestled first and was followed by the next highest weight. The heavyweight was the last wrestler to be on the mat so often it was the heavyweight who determined the winner of the dual match. Mark Tatum had been and always was, no matter what sport, a clutch performer who reveled being in the spotlight.

After college wrestling, Mark took up a new individual type sport and perhaps the toughest of all sports to get really good at…GOLF! Over the years, Tatum became a really good golfer. Just like college wrestling, Mark perfected the basic fundamentals of the game of golf. He had developed a great long game, and like the Dali Lama…he was a big hitter! His short game was only surpassed by his superb putting stroke.

He learned some of his game from his father who was about a two or three handicap player. It is inside this game of golf that Mark has not bested his father in one particular statistic…Aces! Father John Tatum has scored four aces and Mark currently stands at a big fat goose egg! But Dad knows sooner or later, he will get a phone call to report his first ace…it will happen.

Daron Babcock had this to say about his friend and teammate Mark Tatum. "Mark Tatum is the ultimate teammate. He will do anything to help a friend or teammate and would never abandon them in a time of need." He went on and described Tatum as a relentless warrior who feared no one. He added that Tatum went through wrestling partners as fast as Coach Abel could recruit them. Babcock went on to add, "And Tatum didn't just wrestle with them, he tortured them, beat them, and ran them off, one by one and waited patiently for his next victim to abuse on the mat. Mark Tatum was one of the toughest, if not the toughest guys I ever saw! But off the mat, no one was more fun to be around than Mark."

Mark Tatum learned as a member of the Sooner wrestling team from his teammates and Coach Stan Abel the value of helping friends and being a friend a person could count on. So it was only natural that Mark Tatum would follow his father into the insurance business. The question of whether or not Mark Tatum would be a success was a slam dunk type certainty. Mark had virtually succeeded at each and every enterprise he had ever attempted. He began his career as a sales rep for Kansas Farm Bureau Insurance Company in Manhatten, Kansas. He knew just one person in the Kansas town, Kenny Fischer, his wrestling teammate at OU. Mark became one of the best first year agents the company ever had contracted. Just as he had done as a wrestler, he adopted that same relentless effort to learn his new business inside and out. He developed excellent work habits and set increasingly higher and higher goals. Everywhere he went and at every level he advanced to, he achieved outstanding results.

After twenty-five years with his captive company, Mark decided it was time to make a change. The success he had achieved, while excellent and plenty high enough for most, was not enough to satisfy him. Mark Tatum was looking for an opportunity that was truly sky high. He was looking for a game with no limits. After some investigation, he decided that starting an independent agency would be just the challenge he was looking for. So, he formed Tatum Insurance LLC late in 2013. He now has sales reps in Oklahoma, Arizona, California, and Texas. Life is good for Mark and each day brings forth new challenges and new opportunities.

If you are looking for an insurance quote, you might try Tatum Insurance at 405-253-2030 and ask for Mark Tatum.

And to wrap up this wrestling story, a joke about Stan Abel…

Port G. Robertson arguably may have been the staunchest disciplinarian ever in the OU athletic department. His reputation has been well documented. Now enter Port's protégé, Stan Abel. Port had recruited Stan out of Putnam City High School after he had finished 3rd at the Oklahoma State Wrestling Championships. However, Port's keen eye saw something in Abel…the potential to be a great wrestler. Port was not wrong as Stan Abel went on to win two National Championships for Port's Sooner team.

Stan Abel was not only a great wrestler but, without question, he was one of the all-time most flamboyant athletes to ever compete at OU. He pushed Port to the limit with his colorful behavior, yet Port loved the free spirited Abel. In fact, when Port retired as OU's head wrestling coach, he recommended Abel to be his replacement.

Abel, as the head wrestling coach, answered to Port who was in charge of all athletic discipline and often found himself confronted by a plethora of issues created by the antics of the young OU wrestling coach that he loved. One morning Port walked into his office and told Leon Cross, Associate Athletic Director and former OU All American guard in football, "Leon, I was just faced with a great decision as I drove down Jenkins Street. Stan Abel just walked out in front of my car. I was faced with a tough decision…do I hit the brakes or the accelerator?"

How could any Sooner not love Stan Abel…a 110% Sooner and truly cut out of the same cloth as Billy Tubbs and Barry Switzer…all three classic OU coaches who were winners in the Crimson and Cream tradition.

Told to me by my great friend and teammate at OU, Leon Cross.

Mark Tatum—OU Heavyweight Wrestler

SINGLE-SEASON PIN LEADERS

Dan Chaid, 1986	24	Edcar Thomas, 1961	11
Herb Calvert, 1976	18	Wayne Wells, 1966, 1967	11
Edcar Thomas, 1979	15	Dan Hodge, 1956	11
Danny Hodge, 1957	15	John LaViolette, 1986	11
Dan Chaid, 1985	15	Dan Hodge, 1955	10
Joe Melchiore, 1986	13	Frank DeAngelis, 1980	10
Dan Chaid, 1984	12	Mark Tatum, 1986	10
Jeff Callard,	12	Isreal Sheppard, 1982	9
Greg Ruth, 1966	12	Andre Metzger, 1982	9
Andre Metzger, 1980, 1981	11		

Mark and John Tatum—Mark was All-American Big 8 Heavyweight Wrestling champion and won the Bronze Medal in the World Games Sombo Style Wrestling in 1987 in Milan, Italy.

Stan Abel, two time OU All-American and future OU Head Wrestling Coach takes down an opponent

JD ROBERTS—A NEW COACH'S RECORD MAKING DECISION

YOU ALL KNOW HOW I ADMIRE JD ROBERTS—THE MAN WHO SAVED ME from Heavener, OK and gave me the opportunity as an OU football player that turned my life around. You will enjoy this little-known story about JD…

JD left OU and eventually was named the interim head football coach of the New Orleans Saints. He took over in mid season. His team's first opponent was the Detroit Lions. It would prove to be an historic game indeed.

JD's Saints had the ball with only seconds remaining in the contest with Detroit barely ahead, 17-16. The Saints called a time out to discuss strategy with their new head coach. JD suggested they run their "Hail Mary" play since they were 63 yards from a winning field goal. The Saints quarterback informed JD they did not have a "Hail Mary" play. The Saints field goal kicker was standing there and said, "Hell Coach, let me kick a field goal."

JD figured, in the absence of any other good idea, why not? The Saints lined up in field goal formation and the Lions defense, led by All Pro Alex Karras, pointed and laughed as they warned their teammates, "Watch a fake." The ball split the uprights as Tom Dempsey made NFL history with a 63-yard field goal. And secured the first victory as a NFL head coach for the man who brought me to OU.

WAYNE LEE—NOTE TO JOHN

John,

I appreciate your email and I'm sorry I misread or misunderstood the intent of the first email. It is probably more my reading than your writing.

Regarding more directly our playing together at the same position at OU, I would like to make the following comments:

1. It was obvious that you were, and still are, a student of the game of football. You have the perspective of a player, coach, and fan and by your nature know and appreciate a job well done on the field as well as in the classroom.

2. I never had a single doubt of your effort or commitment to do your best on the field at both practice and on the game field.

You also had the ability to demonstrate with your humor and enthusiasm your passion and joy for the game while playing at the highest level.

3. I watched you in practice and in game films and I learned from you and I believe I became a better player as a result of that opportunity.

4. It is interesting as I look back on it that I didn't view our relationship as a competition for the same position as much as an opportunity for both of us to play at our highest level and thus maximize the potential success of our team. There was plenty of room and opportunity for both of us. Our team benefited greatly from both of our contributions.

5. The best that we can do at any undertaking, either mental or physical or both, is do our best at every opportunity. It is difficult for us to know that we have done our best because we always believe we could have done better if we had the opportunity to do it again. I don't think you need to worry about what might have been. You were there and our team benefited greatly.

Will be very interested to read the book. Good luck with it!

GO SOONERS!
Wayne

Note from JET: Wayne Lee was a Co-Captain, along with Leon Cross in 1962. It is said by many different sports coaches that when an athlete practices against great athletes and plays against great athletes, everyone improves. Old JET believes the wisdom in the previous statement.

Wayne Lee was a great athlete and he pushed me every day to become a better player. In the 1961 season, Wayne broke his hand. Because of the substitution rule that limited a player to only enter the game twice in the same quarter, Wayne and I combined to play the rest of the season together and deal with whatever game type situation that arose. This was especially true whenever OU had to punt or kick an extra point or attempt a field goal. These kicking situations created substitution problems for OU because with a broken hand, Wayne could not execute a deep snap.

This unique situation created a situation where it called for team work in the highest possible level. Wayne and I were, if nothing else, great team players willing to do our part in order to achieve success for the team. Wayne Lee is the epitome of class. I always am thrilled anytime I can either talk with my old teammate or be with him on game days. I value his wisdom and especially his friendship.

SOONER FOOTBALL

Wayne Lee, Center #51 with Leon Cross, Guard #61

KJ SANFORD

MY MOTHER REMARRIED IN AUGUST OF 1958. HER NEW HUSBAND AND MY new stepfather was Kenneth James Sanford. Kenneth, as he preferred to be called, would head for Kuwait in the Middle East soon after they were married. He was an expert in constructing oil refineries. So, after a long week he left for a one-year job in the rich Arabian oil fields.

Several months into his stay in Kuwait, a couple of American workers were murdered and all of a sudden Kuwait became a very dangerous place to be. So, in February of 1959, Kenneth Sanford returned to Heavener and the stranger spent each day getting drunk and making my life one of ongoing stress. Kenneth would start each day by downing a six-pack of tall-boy beers. This would be a warm up for a fifth of vodka until he passed out. This behavior would be the SOP pretty much every day.

Eventually, and four or five years after I left Heavener, Lavelle, my mother, delivered the ultimatum. Either quit drinking and get help or hit the road. Kenneth discovered AA and became a star pupil on the One Day at a Time group. He successfully escaped from the bottle. His disease was so completely whipped that the AA ad in the local newspaper read, "If you have a drinking problem, call this number and get help." That telephone number was Kenneth Sanford's number.

Kicking the drinking habit is no easy task and I admired him for doing it. A sober Kenneth Sanford became a great companion for my mother who deserved a happy life. She had raised my sister and me with little to no help.

As I spent more time around Kenneth, I discovered a completely different man than the pain in the butt person he was when drinking. Kenneth was a very intelligent man and more than anything else, he was a bona fide American WW II hero. He was a First Lt. in the US Army Air

Corps, a pilot in the 8th Air Force. Kenneth was the pilot of a B-24 Liberator Bomber. He and his crew were in the first B-24 wing in England.

He and his crew flew 35 missions. He was awarded the Air Corps Flying Medal, European Service Medal, and most notable of all, the Distinguished Flying Cross with three Oak Leaf Clusters, which meant that Sanford was awarded the DFC four times. His first DFC cited Lieutenant Sanford for completing a critical bombing mission even though his B-24 aircraft sustained 119 different flak hits—the smallest the size of a penny and the largest the size of a basketball. No crewmember was wounded despite the number of hits the aircraft took.

On each mission, the losses were around 30% of all aircraft. All of a sudden, I had some real insight into why he drank so much before he saw the light and quit drinking. He was trying to kill the demons living within him. He knew the bombs he was dropping were killing German civilians, including women and children. Plus, can you imagine going out to get into your airplane, knowing that one out of three of the crewmembers on the mission were going to be shot down, killed, or captured that day. And yet in the face of these odds, the young American airmen loaded up, took off into a peril that noncombatants have no idea of what it would be like.

He drank after the war to quell the demons. And why wouldn't he? Against this revelation, I admired his courage even more to crawl out of the alcohol prison that gripped him. Kenneth Sanford never took a drink the rest of his life. He died peacefully, of leukemia. I was by his bed when he died. He and my mother are buried side by side in the Heavener Cemetery.

FINDING HEAVENER, OK

ONE NIGHT THE OU FOOTBALL TEAM WAS RETURNING FROM AN AWAY GAME somewhere, I don't recall where now. Back in the early 60s, the OU football team had not yet discovered jet airline travel; we flew in prop type aircraft.

We were humming along and a flight attendant announced over the intercom system, "For your information, if you will please look out of the left side of the aircraft, we are now passing over Heavener, Oklahoma." I was sitting on the right side of the aircraft and away like a speeding bullet I raced across the aisle, threw back the curtain on the window and below, as far as one could see in any direction, there was one solitary light! Heck, it probably was Heavener. And everyone enjoyed a good chuckle. I probably laughed the most. Everyone on the team knew I was from the small southeastern Oklahoma town of Heavener—that's why they called me the Heavener Flash.

Throughout my life many have asked me how I managed to go from such a small school to such a historic football program like OU. I always have the same answer. Simple, I was just lucky…lucky that we didn't have game films. And my speed was great, but only because of a local geological factor.

At the beginning of most football games, whoever wins the toss usually takes the wind. That is true, but not at Heavener's Doc Harvey Stadium. When the Heavener Wolves would win the toss, we would take the slope. That's right, we wanted to run downhill. When OU asked about my speed in the forty, we gave them the downhill numbers…like 4.3, a real speed merchant. However, the uphill speed was like 8.7. It took a while to get used to a level field at Owen Stadium.

SOONER NATION

SO WHAT MAKES THE SOONER NATION ALL THAT SPECIAL AND DIFFERENT? Or, in the final analysis, is it really all that different? If we examine the history of the Sooner Nation, it would be relatively easy to separate the past almost 100 years of football into three major eras…the Wilkinson, Switzer, and Stoops eras. Each one of those eras would be roughly 15 years duration. Some variance exists, but for comparison purposes, that difference is immaterial.

Each era is marked by a Red Letter event, an event monumental to the extent it stops Sooner Fans in their tracks…something unforgettable, earth shattering!

Let's examine three possibilities, one for each of the three eras, starting with the Wilkinson era. Old JET selects the OU-Nebraska game of 1963. JET was a graduate assistant coach at OU when this event happened. Long time Wilkinson friend and US President John F. Kennedy was assassinated the week of the OU-Nebraska football game. Coach Wilkinson was emotionally devastated; he did not want to play the game. The Nebraska group disagreed and wanted to play. Nebraska prevailed and the game was played, much to the objection of Wilkinson.

This is speculation, however some is factual. How much did the death of his Washington, DC friend affect the Oklahoma head football coach? Think about it sports fans, a few short weeks after losing his friend and a game against rival Nebraska, Coach Wilkinson shocked the Sooner Nation…he resigned!

The news stunned the Sooner Nation. Was this event truly a Red Letter event? Just ask any died in the wool Sooner fan this question, "Hey Bubba, when did Bud resign and retire from coaching?" Chances are a devout member of the Sooner Nation will tell you the week and the year.

Had Coach Wilkinson not decided to retire and enter politics, what would the OU future have become? The answer we will never know. One decision changed everything that one week of Sooner choices at the top.

Next up, The King...Barry Switzer! No doubt about it, Barry brought a certain swagger to the OU Football program. Barry's era reminds old JET of stories about the end of Prohibition in the thirties...Happy Days Are Here Again! Barry changed almost everything except the winning ways Bud had established. Yes Sooner fans, no doubt about it, Bud's boys started a tradition unparalleled in college football. It had been underscored by a still standing 47 straight Sooner wins. But Barry and his boys were equal to the task and matched Bud's three national championships.

In the fifteenth (there about) season, Barry was faced with some acute team problems. Some of his star players were in the news and things were not well in Mecca. Barry took the lion's share of the blame for the behavioral problems some of his team were guilty of. With great sorrow on his part, Switzer offered his resignation, thus ending an unforgettable era of Sooner football.

Barry's popularity remains very high some 20 plus years after the King resigned. And as with Bud, the Sooner Nation, almost to a man, can tell you many memorable Barry Switzer stories. When Barry resigned, his teams had set a new OU winning record, surpassing the Wilkinson era in total wins—and had tied Bud's three national championships. Like the news of Bud's resignation, diehard Sooner fans can tell you where they were when they heard the news that Switzer had retired. This news ended a second Sooner era.

And now for the swan song, the third and final era...the Stoops era. But first an observation. The first era, the Wilkinson Era, was truly and mistakenly Old School Football. Barry ushered in a very different brand of football...Joe Washington, Gregg Pruitt, Keith Jackson, Brian Bosworth style football.

Now enter the Sooner Nation, the Youngstown Flash, Bob Stoops. Stoops would bring to the Sooner Nation a brand of football Sooner fans could not get enough of. It was high octane score a half a hundred on 'em in the first half, win games by the score of 60 to 59 football! In only his second year at the OU football helm, Stoops and his high-powered players had won their first National championship. By his 15th year, Stoops and crew had surpassed both Bud and Barry in total Sooner victories. The third era had happened and the Sooner Nation cried for more.

Then something strange happened. The Stoops Sooners went 8-5 and a strange thing happened on the way to the end of a rival game with in-state team, OSU. It was a Red Letter Event near the end of the game.

Here is the play that stopped the Sooner Nation. It was in the fourth quarter, OU led by four or five points and it was 4th down. The Sooners were in punt formation, the snap was dead on, the punter launched a good punt forcing the OSU deep back, a world class sprinter, and probably the fastest player on both teams, to fair catch the punt.

But hold on there Crimson and Cream breath. OSU is offsides. This was the decision facing OU. If OU declined the penalty, it would be OSU's ball on roughly the ten or fifteen-yard line. OSU would have the ball with almost 90 yards or so to go and only slightly over one minute left in the game, with OU leading. Then, up jumps Jasper, and OU elected to take the penalty, forcing OU to punt again with the dangerous and faster than a New York minute sprinter deep to receive the re-punt. OU's punter boomed a long punt which was too good, OSU's sprinter caught the punt, made a couple of Sooner's miss, then got a good block or two, went the distance, and OSU upset the favored Sooners…snatching from the jaws of defeat to victory over their arch rivals from Sooner Land.

Against that backdrop of information, I submit to you evidence that the Sooner Nation is truly special. There is no one like us—Sooner Born and Bred—Sooners.

Ever since that fateful day that we lost to the Aggies of OSU, when Nancy Jean and Old JET enter a restaurant and we spy members of the Sooner Nation sitting at a table sporting a Sooner hat of shirt, JET sashays over to their table and says, "Excuse me folks, but I have a question I would like to ask you. Do you mind? It will only take a second or two to answer."

Being naturally polite, the Sooner Nation citizens always say, "Well sure, what is it you need to ask us?"

Then I spring the $64,000 question on them, "So, would you have taken the penalty and punted again or refused the penalty and made the Aggies march almost 90 yards with just a tad over one minute in the game?" So far, 100% have said, refuse the penalty!

Every true member of the Sooner Nation can answer that question, with no explanation necessary. That is what makes the Sooner Nation special. Even little old ladies answer the question. And that is why I love to write about Sooners. There are none like us.

Boomer Sooner and thus ends the story about the three eras. Bob Stoops is still our hero, and the Sooner Nation is behind all of our coaches, win or tie.

Old JET had an email from one of my many Sooner fans. It was a young man asking his father what a loser was. His father replied, "I don't know, Son, we are Sooners!"

President John F. Kennedy and Bud Wilkinson, 23 March 1961, when Bud was named director of Youth Fitness Program in the Oval Office of the White House. Photo compliments of Kennedy Library and Museum

Barry Switzer

Sooner Football Coach Bob Stoops

ABOUT THE AUTHOR

JOHN E. TATUM, CALLED JOHNNY TATUM BY THOSE HE GOT TO KNOW AT OU, grew up in the foothills of the Ozarks in southeastern Oklahoma. He attended Heavener High School where he excelled in sports. He was a three-year letterman in football, basketball, and baseball. His senior year in high school, he earned Special Recognition on the 1958 Oklahoma High School All-State football team. He was the captain of the All-Conference football team and named the MVP award winner.

In later years, Tatum was named to the Daily Oklahoman All-Decade Oklahoma 1950s football team, and in 2007, Oklahoma's centennial year, Tatum was named by the Daily Oklahoman sports editor as the best football player to have played at Heavener High School for the past 100 years. Tatum played center and inside linebacker at OU under the legendary Bud Wilkinson, was a three-year letterman, and received awards for outstanding defensive play.

After graduating with a degree in Education from OU, Tatum coached and taught high school biology for six years. In 1968, Tatum coached the Star Spencer Bobcats baseball team to the first state championship for any sport at Star Spencer High School. He earned Coach of the Year Award and also was named in 1969 as a recipient of the Jaycees Outstanding Young Educator Award.

In 1970, Tatum left teaching and coaching and went into business selling insurance. His insurance career spanned four decades with the Farm Bureau Insurance Companies. Tatum started his career in Durant, Oklahoma where he helped start a little league football program. From Durant, Tatum rescued a failing Farm Bureau Agency in Tucson, Arizona. Following that successful venture in Tucson, Tatum moved to Fargo, North Dakota and spent five years building and developing a full time Farm Bureau sales force in the state. Tatum moved from North Dakota to Lincoln, Nebraska where he served five years as the state sales manager for the Farm Bureau Insurance Company of Nebraska.

In December of 1987, Tatum was promoted to the position of CEO. In 2002, Tatum was selected to head up a multiple company merger that included Farm Bureau Companies in Iowa, Nebraska, Kansas, Utah, Arizona, Kansas, Minnesota, South Dakota, and New Mexico.

Tatum served on Nebraska State Guarantee Fund as Chairman, Chairman of the Nebraska Federation of Insurance Companies, Lincoln Arts Council Board of Directors, and the Lincoln Symphony Board of Directors. Tatum also served on the Advisory Council of the American Agriculture Reinsurance Company in Park Ridge, Illinois. In 2004, Tatum retired from Farm Bureau Financial Insurance companies as Senior Vice President of Farm Bureau Mutual Insurance Company.

John Tatum and his wife Nancy Jean Tatum have six children, Mark Tatum, Robert Tatum, Monica Bolin, Penny Dee Bigelow, Marilee Dose, and Sam Marshall. And grandchildren, Kelsey Tatum, Jake Tatum, Isabella Tatum, Davis Bigelow, Summerslee Latham, Sterling Latham, Daryan Marshall, and Myla Jean Marshall.